SELECTED POEMS

SELECTED POEMS

With an Essay on her own Poetry

by

EDITH SITWELL

Boston

HOUGHTON MIFFLIN COMPANY

1937

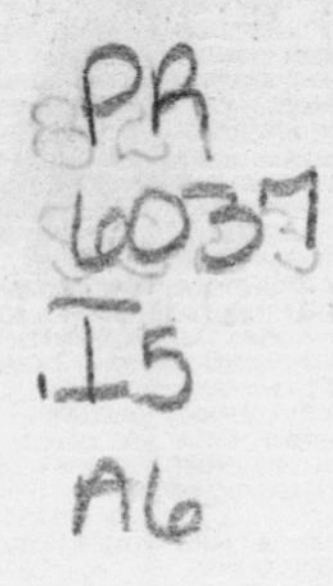

Made and Printed in Great Britain by the KEMP HALL PRESS, LTD.
in the City of Oxford

CONTENTS

SOME NOTES ON MY OWN POETRY

For John Sparrow

In every age we find poets discussing the problems of poetry, defending their verses and giving reasons for innovations in various Prefaces and Defences of Poetry. Thomas Lodge, for instance, published a *Defence of Plays* in 1580, and Sir Philip Sidney an *Apologie for Poetrie* about the year 1595; Ben Jonson treated of the problems of Poetry in his *Discoveries*, and Thomas Campion wrote his *Observations on the Art of English Poesie* in 1602. It may not therefore seem out of place or the result of an undue vanity, if I gather together these notes in the hope of dispelling in the mind of a few readers some of the delusions that have arisen round what is amongst the most misunderstood poetry of our time.

It was only to be expected that hostility would be aroused by these poems, since from a sensuous point of view (and technically in certain poems) I was breaking new ground; and of this hostility I do not complain; I do, however, complain that many well-meaning persons have attributed to my poems qualities which are not inherent in them.

I was brought up in the country, and mine is a country world. The artificiality of which my poems are accused is such that when I write of emotion I try to strip the passion down to the barest possible expression, a quintessential simplicity. When my poems deal with emotion, they are always the most simple and primitive emotions of simple and primitive people, as in "The Heart and the Hambone," and "The Little Ghost who died for Love." I write of a dead girl returning to the world in spring, or of the broken heart of a girl whose love was betrayed for the sake of a harlot, weeping for one who, living, was yet:

> "This Dead, who fell that he might satisfy
> The hungry grave's blind need,—
>
> "That Venus stinking of the Worm!"

I write of the mother who, murdered by her son, yet, in the darkness of death, remembers that

> "Once Judas had a childish kiss
> And still his mother knows but this."

and of the man whose dead love returned to warm him with her kiss.

I was born by the wildest seas that England knows, and my earliest recollection is of the tides, the wild rush of waves, the sweep onward, heard night and day, so that it seemed the sound of one's own blood. This sound is heard in many of the lines in "The Four Elegies," and in "Gold Coast Customs"; in such lines, for instance, as these from "The Heart and the Hambone":

> "How shall I know you from the other long
> Anguishing grave-worms? I can but foretell
> The worm where once the kiss clung, and that last less
> chasm-deep farewell."

wherein the pauses seem those of waves about to break, followed by the rush onward of the sea.

II

Much of the trouble that has arisen about my poetry is due to the fact that the members of the Bungalow School of Verse do not recognize the country when they see it, since they are far too busy making an irritating noise with their motor-bicycles, that are always being wound up and that never start.

The vegetable world to them signifies an aspidistra; to me it is a world where the:

> " . . . swan-skin leaves of cherries seem a cloud
> Where coral tears of the rich light fall loud
> In that smooth darkness; the gourds dark as caves
> Hold thick gold honey for their fountain waves;
>
> Figs dark and wrinkled as Silenus hold
> Rubies and garnets, and the melons cold
> Waves like a fountain; falling on the grass
> The apples boom like sharp green summer rain."

We all have a right to our own tastes.

The world I see is a country world, a universe of growing things, where magic and growth are one, and wherein, as in George Peele's lines:

> " God in the whizzing of a pleasant wind
> Shall march upon the tops of mulberry trees; "

a world of rough fruitful suns, and the age of the innocence of man—of the forests

> " Where the wolf Nature from maternal breast
> Fed us with strong brown milk. . . ."

the age

> " When Time's vast sculptures from rough dust began,
> And natural law and moral were but one,—
> Derived from the rich wisdom of the sun.

In those deep ages the most primitive
And roughest and uncouthest shapes did live
Knowing the memory of before their birth,
And their soul's life before this uncouth earth.

We could remember in that ancient time
Of our primeval innocence, a clime
Divined deep in the soul, in which the light
Of vaster suns gave wisdom to our sight."

Sometimes we find poems whose movement is like the growth of a slower plant-life, as in these lines from " Romance ":

" When the green century of summer rains
Lay on the leaves, then like the rose I wept.
For I had dwelt in sorrow as the rose
In the deep heaven of her leaves lies close.
Then you, my gardener, with green fingers stroked my leaves
Till all the gold drops turned to honey. Grieves
This empire of green shade when honeyed rains
And amber blood flush all the sharp green veins
Of the rich rose?
So doth my rose-shaped heart
Feel the first flush of summer; love's first smart
Seemed no more sorrowful than the deep tears
The rose wept in that green and honeyed clime."

Here the ethereal quality of the plant-world, the slow growth of the plant, the colour and scent of the rose are conveyed by the different wave-lengths of the vowels.

At other moments, as a contrast to this world, we find one of heavy, brutish, greedy darkness:

"... the countrysides where people know
That Destiny is wingless and bemired,
With feathers dirty as a hen's, too tired
To fly—where old pig-snouted Darkness grovels
For life's mired rags among the broken hovels——"

or a countryside where everything we see is a symbol of something beyond the world, but where the people live the life of growing things rooted deeply in the mould, and understanding only the world of the unawakened senses, and not the significance of their language—seeing the stars as no more remote than the flowers in their own potting-sheds, and the vast and unknown splendours as something homely, so that death and the eternal stars are no more strange.

"It seemed a low-hung country of the blind,—
A sensual touch upon the heart and mind,
Like crazy creaking chalets hanging low
From the dark hairiness of bestial skies
The clouds seem, like a potting-shed where grow
The flower-like planets for the gay flower-show:
Gold-freckled calceolarias,
Marigolds, cinerarias,
African marigolds, coarse-frilled,
And cherries, apricots, all chilled
With dew, for thus the bright stars seemed
To cottage windows where none dreamed,
But country gentlemen who from their birth,
Like kind red strawberries, root deep in earth
And sleep as in the grave, dream far beyond
The sensual aspects of the hairy sky
That something hides, they have forgotten why!
And so they wander, aiming with their gun
At mocking feathered creatures that have learnt
That movement is but groping into life,—
Under rough trees like shepherds' goatish tents."

To this countryside, Death comes, not as a world-enveloping shade, but as :

" . . . goat-footed mincing Death."

a bucolic skeleton, with a clattering, hard footfall, a rustic god, a satyr waiting for Beauty beneath the trees.

In most of the Bucolic Comedies, there are no technical experiments, and usually the rhythm is a drone-sound like that of a hive or the wind in the trees. Some of the poems, again, have a goat-footed, rustic sound, deliberately uncouth—a hard quick uncouth rhythm—so that it seems as if we are not listening to the peasants' boots falling on a soft soil, but to the far earlier sound of satyr-hooves falling on a ground that is hard with winter, or harsh and sharp with spring, or mad and harsh with summer—or, to quote Rimbaud, to " the eclogues in sabots, grunting in the orchards."

At moments, the shortness and roundness of the lines produce the effect of small uncouth buds breaking from the earth—daisy-buds for instance; or they spurt like a hard shrill jet of water, as in the shorter lines of

GARDENER JANUS CATCHES A NAIAD.

" Baskets of ripe fruit in air
The bird-songs seem, suspended where,

Between the hairy leaves, trills dew,
All tasting of fresh green anew.

Ma'am, I've heard your laughter flare
Through your waspish-gilded hair:

Feathered masks,
Pots of peas,
Janus asks
Naught of these.
Creaking water
Brightly stripèd,
Now I've caught her—
Shrieking biped.
Flute sounds jump
And turn together,
Changing clumps
Of glassy feather.
In among the
Pots of peas
Naiad changes—
Quick as these."

In one of the Bucolic Comedies, " Early Spring," the effect of windless cold, of that time of waiting and watching when the first buds are spurting from the dark boughs, and when the winter is about to change into spring—these sensations are produced by the absolute stillness of the lines, the faintness of the pauses when they occur—(and they are very rare, excepting at the end of lines).

The wooden chalets of the cloud
Hang down their dull blunt ropes to shroud

Red crystal bells upon each bough
(Fruit-buds that whimper). No winds slough

Our faces, furred with cold like red
Furred buds of satyr springs, long dead.

The cold wind creaking in my blood
Seems part of it, as grain of wood;

Among the coarse goat-locks of snow
Mamzelle still drags me, to and fro;

Her feet make marks like centaur hoofs
In hairy snow; her cold reproofs

Die, and her strange eyes look oblique
As the slant crystal buds that creak.

If she could think me distant, she
In the snow's goat-locks certainly

Would try to milk those teats, the buds,
Of their warm sticky milk—the cuds

Of strange long-past fruit-hairy springs—
Beginnings of first earthy things!"

There are, indeed, only two long pauses to be found *within* the lines—one after "whimper," because the second syllable dies away like a little cold air; the other after "milk," because this is a word of one syllable and a fraction, and this extra fraction being incredibly faint, the effect is not that of a flutter, or a movement, but of a tiny pause.

Any other definite movement in this poem is caused by words ending in "d" being placed in close juxtaposition—slowing the lines:

"Our faces furre*d* with col*d* like re*d*
Furre*d* bu*d*s of satyr springs long *dead*.

The col*d* win*d* creaking in my bloo*d*
Seems part of it, as grain of woo*d*"—

and by the unmuted "r"s in the above lines and in

some others, which give the faintest possible movement, like that of a bough stirring in the air.

Such other pauses as occur, so faint as to be almost imperceptible, give the lines a strange chilliness, all the stranger because the " o " and " ou " sounds throughout the poem (when they are not sharp with spring, as in " cloud," " shroud," " bough," " slough ") are warm—give the impression of growing things waiting beneath the hard soil in the darkness, till the winter shall be gone. A poignant cold air creeps from time to time into these lines, with the sharp freezing " e " sounds, while the subtle faint change from the cold wind to the swaddled warmth of the growing things waiting beneath the hard soil, these are conveyed by the varying lengths and depths of these " o " and " ou " sounds, sometimes dulling and shrinking as with cold into a " u " that is only a shrunken echo of these—as in the couplet:

> " The wooden chalets of the cloud
> Hang down their d*u*ll bl*u*nt ropes to shroud."

The feeling of cold air comes, too, with an occasional dissonance, as in the " dull," " crystal," " bells " sounds of the first two couplets. The subtle variations which lie between the dissonances and assonances, as well as the faint pauses, do, indeed, give a slight movement. " Blunt," for instance, is faintly higher, longer, more numb with cold than is " dull," " bells " is slightly longer than " red," " buds " is sharper yet rounder, and less dark than " furred." And these, as well, gather together the rhythm, whilst conveying the sense of this time of waiting.

In many of these poems the subject is the growth of

consciousness. Sometimes it is that of a person who has always been blind, and who, suddenly endowed with sight, must *learn* to see; or it is the cry of that waiting, watching world, where everything we see is a symbol of something beyond, to the consciousness that is yet buried in this earth-sleep; and it is this that we find in "Aubade," a poem which, on its first appearance, was held to contain obscurities which were insuperable:

"Jane, Jane,
Tall as a crane,
The morning light creaks down again.

Comb your cockscomb-ragged hair,
Jane, Jane, come down the stair.

Each dull, blunt wooden stalactite
Of rain creaks, hardened by the light,

Sounding like an overtone
From some lonely world unknown.

But the creaking, empty light
Will never harden into sight,

Will never penetrate your brain
With overtones like the blunt rain.

The light would show, if it could harden,
Eternities of kitchen garden.

Cockscomb flowers that none will pluck,
And wooden flowers that 'gin to cluck.

In the kitchen you must light
Flames as staring, red and white,

As carrots or as turnips—shining
Where the cold dawn light lies whining.

Cockscomb hair on the cold wind
Hangs limp, turns the milk's weak mind.

Jane, Jane,
Tall as a crane,
The morning light creaks down again."

In the third and last line I said "creaks" because, in a very early dawn, after rain, the light has a curious uncertain quality, as though it does not run quite smoothly. Also, it falls in hard cubes, squares, and triangles, which, again, give one the impression of a creaking sound, because of the association with wood. As for the lines

"Each dull, blunt wooden stalactite
Of rain creaks, hardened by the light,"

in the early dawn, long raindrops are transformed by the light, until they have the light's own quality of hardness, also they have the dull and blunt and tasteless quality of wood; as they move in the wind, they seem to creak.

"Sounding like an overtone
From some lonely world unknown."

Though it seems to us as though we heard them sensorily, yet the sound is unheard in reality; it has the quality of an overtone from some unknown and mysterious world.

"But the creaking, empty light
Will never harden into sight,

Will never penetrate your brain
With overtones like the blunt rain."

The poem is about a country servant, a girl on a farm, plain and neglected and unhappy, and with a sad bucolic stupidity, coming down in the dawn to light the fire; and this phrase means that to her mind the light is an empty thing which conveys nothing. It cannot bring sight to her—she is not capable of seeing anything; it can never bring overtones to her mind, because she is not capable of hearing them. She scarcely knows even that she is suffering.

"The light would show, if it could harden,
Eternities of kitchen garden,

Cockscomb flowers that none will pluck,
And wooden flowers that 'gin to cluck."

If she were capable of seeing anything, still she would only see the whole of eternity as the world of kitchen gardens to which she is accustomed, with flowers red and lank as cockscombs (uncared for, just as she is uncared for), and those hard flowers that dip and bend beneath the rain till they look (and seem as though they must sound) like hens clucking.

"In the kitchen you must light
Flames as staring, red and white,

As carrots or as turnips—shining
Where the cold dawn light lies whining."

To me the shivering movement of a certain cold

dawn light upon the floor suggests a kind of high animal whining or whimpering, a half-frightened and subservient urge to something outside our consciousness.

> " Cockscomb hair on the cold wind
> Hangs limp, turns the milk's weak mind."

is obviously a joke, and a joke may be permitted even to a poet.

Sometimes we find a consciousness awakening from sleep, seeing, with a clearer, sharper vision than that of the ordinary sense dulled with custom—piercing down to the essence of the thing seen, knowing that the ephemeral six-rayed snowflake is the counterpart of the six-rayed crystal in its eternity—seeing that:

> " . . . all things have beginnings; the bright plume
> Was once thin grass, in shady winter's gloom.
>
> And the furred fire is barking for the shape
> Of hoarse-voiced animals; cold air agape
>
> Whines to be shut in water's shape and plumes;"

and so guessing at the immense design of the world, " the correspondences whereby men may speak with angels."

Sometimes, again, it is the fumbling of the unawakened consciousness towards a higher state, and sometimes it is a purely animal consciousness—the beginning of all earthy things.

Thus, a flower, in " Springing Jack," is a

> " Clear angel face on hairy stalk;
> (Soul grown from flesh, an ape's young talk.)"

" Dark Song " is a poem about the beginning of things, and their relationship—the fire that purrs like an animal and has a beast's thick coat (the crumbling furry black coal), a girl whose blood has the dark pulse and instincts of the earth:

> " The fire was furry as a bear
> And the flames purr . . .
> The brown bear rambles in his chain,
> Captive to cruel men,
> Through the dark and hairy wood . . .
> The maid sighed: ' All my blood
> Is animal. They thought I sat
> Like a household cat;
> But through the dark woods rambled I . . .
> Oh, if my blood would die! '
> The fire had a bear's fur ;
> It heard and knew . . .
> The dark earth, furry as a bear,
> Grumbled too! "

The long, harsh, animal-purring " r "s and the occasional double-vowels, as in " bear " and " fire," though these last are divided by a muted " r," convey the uncombatable animal instinct. The poem is built on a scheme of harsh " r "s, alternating with dulled " r "s, and the latter, with the thickness of the " br " and the " mb "s in:

> " The brown bear rambles in his chain."

give the thickness of the bear's dull fur. The subtle dissonances of the first line:

> " The fire was furry as a bear "

the one-and-a-half syllables, stretching forward and

upward and then breaking, of " fire," contrasted with the dark thick numb insistence of the first syllable in " furry,"—the fact that the dissonances ending the first six lines are *dropping* dissonances—this conveys the feeling of the animal's thick paws that have not the power of lifting. The sinking or dulled dissonances, which end some of the lines in the place of rhymes, " bear" " fur"—" chain" " men"—the way in which, in the midst of this darkness, there is an occasional high insistent vowel-sound, these effects are deliberate, and are meant to convey a darkened groping. Only once is there a rising dissonance (again purposeful) and that is towards the end of the poem.

If some of the images in these poems appear strange, it is because my senses are like those of primitive peoples, at once acute and uncovered—and they are interchangeable; where the language of one sense is insufficient to convey a meaning, a sensation, I use another, and by this means, I attempt to pierce down to the essence of the thing seen, producing or heightening its significance by discovering in it attributes which at first sight seem alien, but which are actually related—by producing its quintessential colour (sharper, brighter, than that seen by an eye grown stale), and by stripping it of all unessential details. The apparent strangeness comes, too, from the fact that all expression is welded into an image, not removed into a symbol that is inexact, or squandered into a metaphor.

It is this compression, this heightening of the colour into one more piercing, which makes such lines as these, from " Metamorphosis " appear, at first sight, difficult :

"The dark green country temple of the snows
Hides porphyry bones of nymphs whence grew the rose

And dark green dog-haired leaves of strawberries,
All marked with maps of unknown lands and seas,

And that small negro page, the cross dark quail,
Chasing the ghosts of dairymaids that fail

In butter-yellow dew by Georgian stables,
(The snow, dark green as strawberry leaves, has gables.)"

This mention of nymphs is produced frequently, as a proof of my intense artificiality. But can it really be claimed that they are not as useful and interesting as protagonists, as pretty little Mrs. Perkins or that youthful follower of the doctrines of Marx, Mr. Simpson, who, under one guise or another, are the fashionable protagonists of most of the poems that are being written to-day? And in any case, I use them only as an embodiment of:

"Strange long past fruit-hairy springs,
Beginnings of first earthy things."

In "Père Amelot," which is a poem about an unawakened being, whose death, sharp and sudden, and inflicted for no purpose, leaves him nodding in his nightcap as he had done throughout his life—the image "hen-cackling grass," refers to quaker-grass, and it was suggested by the fact that the colour and dustiness of the pods are like the colour and dustiness of a hen, are dry, and have markings like those on a hen's legs, and, as well, by the fact that the shaking movement resembles, for me at least, the quick dry sound and dipping movement of a hen cackling. In another poem, the lines:

> " Hoarse as a dog's bark
> The heavy leaves are furred "

is a reference to the sharp way in which certain leaves jut from their branches—and their rough furry, yet sharp quality. The young leaves of the chestnut-tree spring from their branches in just that way, and are thickly bunched, too, and rough, yet sharp. In the same poem, the line:

> " Furred is the light "

refers to misty moonlight.

As for the image in another poem, about " pigeons smelling of ginger-bread," in the summer, when their feathers are hot from the sun, they *do* smell like ginger-bread, and I am afraid there is nothing to be done about it.

I know, however, that this method of intense concentration of an image leads, sometimes, to difficulties, and that the writer must beware of producing an image which is purely personal—since the aim should be to increase the general consciousness. Readers have, I think, a right to complain of the obscurity of the following line from Section XIV of " The Sleeping Beauty ":

> " Far off, the Martha-coloured scabious "

since it is the result of a personal memory, and is not part of the general experience, and I must not, therefore, feel resentment if the line is not understood. As a child, I had a nursery-maid called Martha, who always wore a smocked and honeycombed gown of cashmere exactly the colour of a scabious. These flowers, too, look like cashmere, and they look as if they were smocked and honeycombed. " Emily-coloured primulas," however, in the poem called " Spring " came into my mind simply because Emily is a very bucolic name, and primulus remind me of the bright pink cheeks of country girls. On the same page as that in which the line about the Martha coloured scabious appears, we find:

> " And underneath the cotton-nightcap trees
> Wanders a little cold pig-snouted breeze."

The first line refers to trees covered closely with white flowers, and having a sleepy look, whilst in the second line I have tried to evoke the feeling of a soft blunt breeze, very rustic.

The poems in " Façade " are, for the most part, abstract patterns, difficult technical experiments. Some deal with materialism, and the world crumbling into dust, some have as protagonists shadows, or ghosts, moving, not in my country world, but in a highly mechanical universe; others have beings moving

> " To the small sound of Time's drum in the heart,"

figures gesticulating against the darkness, from the warmth and light of their little candle-show.

The technical experiments are in the nature of inquiries into the effect on rhythm, and on speed, of the use of rhymes, assonances and dissonances, placed outwardly, at different places in the line, in most elaborate patterns; and in the effect on speed of the use of equivalent syllables, that system which produces almost more variations than any other device.

The rhythm and speed of a skilful unrhymed poem

differ from the rhythm and speed of a rhymed poem containing the same number of feet, and both the rhymed and the unrhymed poems differ slightly in these respects from a poem ending with assonances or dissonances, but containing the same number of feet. Again, assonances and dissonances put at different places within the lines and intermingled with equally skilfully-placed internal rhymes, have an immense effect upon rhythm and speed; and their effect on rhythm, and sometimes, but not always, on speed, is different from that of lines containing elaborately schemed internal rhymes without assonances or dissonances. And how slight, how subtle, are the changes of speed or of depth in English poetry due to differences in texture, and due to the fact that the English, in their cunning over the matter of poetry, have adopted the idea of equivalence. For is it really to be supposed that two words of one syllable each, equal in speed one word of two syllables? The two-syllabled words, if unweighted by heavy consonants, move far more quickly. The system therefore of equivalent syllables gives variation, as we shall see when we come to examine a poem called "Fox Trot," later in this essay.

"Said King Pompey"—a poem about materialism and the triumphant dust, is, like "Dark Song," built on a scheme of "r"s, but there the use and the effect is wholly different, for this poem is not formed on a scheme of alternate harsh and muted "r"s, as in "Dark Song;" instead, the "r"s with the faint elision which in this case results from them, give the effect of dust fluttering from the ground, or of the beat of a dying heart:

"Said King Pompey, the emperor's ape,
Shuddering black in his temporal cape
Of dust: 'The dust is everything—
The heart to love and the voice to sing,
Indianapolis,
And the Acropolis,
Also the hairy sky that we
Take for a coverlet comfortably' . . .
Said the Bishop
Eating his ketchup:—
'There still remains Eternity
Swelling the diocese'—
That elephantiasis,
The flunkeyed and trumpeting Sea!"

In the first two lines, the sound rises. "Pompey," in sound, is a dark distorted shadow of "Emperor" and its crouching echo, "temporal"—a shadow upside down, one might say, for in "emperor" the sound dies down in hollow darkness, whereas in "Pompey" it begins in thick muffling animal darkness, and then rises, dying away into a little thin whining air. The crazy reversed sound "Indianapolis," "Acropolis"—(Acropolis being a hollow darkened echo of Indianapolis, broken down, and toppling over into the abyss)—this effect is deliberate.

It is admissable that certain arrangements of words ending in "ck" (black, quack, duck, clack, etc.) cast little almost imperceptible shadows. In "The Bat," a poem about the waiting, watching world of the Shade, I have contrasted these shadows, so small yet so menacing, with those flat and shadeless words that end with "t" and with "d," experimenting too, as do all poets, with the different vibrations to be gained from the alternate use of poignant, dark, and flat " a " sounds:

" Castellated, tall
From battlements fall
Shades on heroic
Lonely grass,
Where the moonlight's echoes die and pass.
Near the rustic boorish,
Fustian Moorish,
Castle wall of the ultimate Shade,
With his cloak castellated as that wall, afraid,
The mountebank doctor,
The old stage quack,
Where decoy duck dust
Began to clack,
Watched Heliogabalusene the Bat
In his furred cloak hang head down from the flat
Wall, cling to what is convenient,
Lenient.
' If you hang upside down with squeaking shrill,
You will see dust, lust, and the will to kill,
And life is a matter of which way falls
Your tufted turreted Shade near these walls,
For muttering guttering shadow will plan
If you're ruined wall, or pygmy man,'
Said Heliogabalusene: ' or a pig,
Or the empty Caesar in tall periwig.'
And the mountebank doctor,
The old stage quack,
Spread out a black membraned wing of his cloak
And his shuffling footsteps seem to choke,
Near the Castle wall of the ultimate Shade
Where decoy duck dust
Quacks, clacks, afraid."

In this poem, some of the " a "s and the " u "s

have neither depth nor body, are flat and death-rotten, yet at times, the words in which they occur cast a small menacing shadow because of the " ck " endings, though frequently these shadows are followed almost immediately by flatter, deader, more shadeless words ending in " t " or in " d."

> " Where decoy du*ck* dus*t*
> Beg*a*n to cl*ack*
> Watched Helioga*ba*lusene the B*a*t
> In his furred cloak h*a*ng head down from the fl*a*t
> Wall," etc.

The only body in the first three lines of this quotation (if we except the round second syllable of " decoy ") is in the consonants (casting those little threatening shadows), of " duck " and " clack." In the lines :

> " Shades on heroic
> Lonely grass,
> Where the moonlight's echoes die and pass,
> Near the rustic boorish
> Fustian Moorish
> Castle wall of the ultimate Shade,"

the long " o "s of " heroic " and " lonely," cast at opposite ends of two succeeding lines (" lonely " being slightly longer than " heroic ")—the still deeper " oo " of " moonlight," the hollow sound of " echoes " —these throw long, and opposed, shadows, and in the case of " heroic " and " echoes," these seem broken columns of shade. The " oo " in " boorish " and " Moorish " are still darker than these, and the shadows seem at once blown forward by the " r "s, as by a gust of wind, and broken by these. " Rustic," " fustian " and " ultimate " are broken echoes of each other ; but " rustic " is harder than the other echoes, because of the " c," and is less wavering and indeterminate. The varying length and depth of the " a " sounds in:

" Castle wall of the ultimate Shade,
With his cloak castellated as that wall, afraid."

give a sense of fear, of something which alternately tries to shrink away into the darkness, and to rear itself up as in self-protection: The long second " a " in " castellated " (coming after the huddled beginning of the word) and its exact counterpart, the second " a " of " afraid," coming after the short crouching first " a " and the shuddering " fr "—these, falling in their particular places in the line, give a feeling that the half unreal figure of the old stage quack (the Bat's half human counterpart)—a figure which is so flat and empty that its only reality seems to lie in the slightly thicker, muffling cloak sound of " mountebank," and whose shadow, he being part and parcel of the Shade, is not the shadow cast by a man, but like small menacing shadows which prophesy of the ultimate darkness—this figure seems raising itself up to its full height as if fearing attack.

In the line:

" The old stage quack,"

the word " stage," with its crumbling " ge," is a reversed, dry, and crumbling echo or shadow of the " sh " of " shade," and in that word we have already the beginning of the death-like rottenness which will be completed by the dull " a " and the shades cast by the " ck " in " quack."

The poem called " The Drum," which belongs neither to the world of " Façade," nor to that of

" Bucolic Comedies," but to a night-world which lies between, is founded on a story told by that very odd clergyman the Reverend Joseph Glanvil, chaplain to King Charles II, in his records of witches and witchcraft. It contains, at the beginning, certain of the same experiments as are to be found in " The Bat," but in " The Drum " the rhythm and the variations in this are infinitely more complicated:

" In his tall senatorial
Black and manorial
House where decoy-duck
Dust doth clack—
Clatter and quack
To a shadow black,—
Said the musty Justice Mompesson;
'What is that dark stark beating drum
That we hear rolling like the sea?'
'It is a beggar with a pass
Signed by you.' 'I signed not one.'
They took the ragged drum that we
Once heard rolling like the sea;
In the house of the Justice it must lie
And usher in Eternity.

. . . . .

Is it black night?
Black as Hecate howls a star
Wolfishly, and whined
The wind from very far.

In the pomp of the Mompesson house is one
Candle that lolls like the midnight sun,
Or the coral comb of a cock; . . . it rocks . . .
Only the goatish snow's locks
Watch the candles lit by fright
One by one through the black night.

Through the kitchen there runs a hare—
Whinnying, whines like grass, the air;
It passes; now is standing there
A lovely lady . . . see her eyes—
Black angels in a heavenly place,
Her shady locks and her dangerous grace.

'I thought I saw the wicked old witch in
The richest gallipot in the kitchen!'
A lolloping galloping candle confesses.
'Outside in the passage are wildernesses
Of darkness rustling like witches' dresses.'

Out go the candles one by one,
Hearing the rolling of a drum!

What is the march we hear groan
As the hoofèd sound of a drum marched on
With a pang like darkness, with a clang
Blacker than an orang-outang?
'Heliogabalus is alone,—
Only his bones to play upon!'

The mocking money in the pockets
Then turned black . . . now caws
The fire . . . outside, one scratched the door
As with iron claws,—

Scratching under the children's bed
And up the trembling stairs . . . 'Long dead'
Moaned the water black as crape.
Over the snow the wintry moon
Limp as henbane, or herb paris,
Spotted the bare trees; and soon

Whinnying, neighed the maned blue wind
Turning the burning milk to snow,
Whining it shied down the corridor—
Over the floor I heard it go
Where the drum rolls up the stair, nor tarries."

In the first few lines, the sense of menace, of deepening darkness, is conveyed by the dissonances, so subtle they might almost be assonances, of " tall," " senatorial," " manorial," the " o " of " senatorial " being deeper than the dissonantal " a " in " tall." " Black," " duck," " clack," " clatter " and " quack," with their hard consonants and dead vowels are dry as dust, and the deadness of dust is conveyed thus, and, as well, by the dulled dissonance to the " a "s, of the " u " in " duck " followed by its still more crumbling assonance " dust." (By " decoy-duck dust " I mean very thick dry dust. A duck's quacking is, to me, one of the driest of sounds, and it has a peculiar deadness.)

The sharp and menacing rhythm of the first four lines is given by the fact that " black " in the second line is at the opposite side from " duck " and " clack " in the fourth and fifth, and this throws reversed shadows. In the lines:

" Clatter and quack
To a shadow black "

" Clatter," coming, as it does, immediately after " clack " has an odd sound like that of a challenge thrown down in an empty place by one who, having offered it, then shrinks away in fear. It is a fact that the second syllable of " clatter," instead of casting a shadow, shrinks away into itself and dies. Its flatness is of a different quality to the flatness of the word

" shadow," which is less dead, but still more bodiless —more bodiless because the " d " is less thick than the two " t "s—less dead because the last syllable has the length and depth of the dark vowel sound.

In the line:

> " Said the musty Justice Mompesson:
> What is that dark stark beating drum?"

the thick assonances of " musty Justice," the rhymes " dark stark " placed so closely together, produce a menacing echo. These latter do not leap into the air, as do the rhymes placed immediately together in " Fox Trot," for the reason that in " Fox Trot " they have light and bodiless endings, whilst in " The Drum " they are weighed down by the shadow-casting " k"s.

We find, occasionally, subtle variations of thickness and thinness (and consequently variations of darkness) brought about in assonances and rhymes by the changing of a consonant or labial, from word to word, as in the first two lines of the poem, where the grave darkness of " senatorial " changes to the thicker, more impenetrable " manorial," which for all its thickness is hollow, and in the seventh line—(here it is the case of a distorted dissonance)—where the fat sloth of " musty Justice " changes to the thick black muffled bulk and darkness of " Mompesson." Again, in the twentieth and twenty-first lines:

> " In the pomp of the Mompesson house is one
> Candle that lolls like a midnight sun "

the round body and concentration of " pomp " is changed to the softness and shapelessness of " lolls," whilst in:

"Out go the candles one by one,
Hearing the rolling of a drum."—

we have the change from the disembodied sound of "one" with its faint echo, to the thickness of "drum" wherein darkness takes on a body. In the lines:

"Black as Hecate howls a star
Wolfishly, and whined
The wind from very far."

the small-vowelled, quick three-syllabled word "Hecate" makes the line rock up and down. In the next line, the word "wolfishly" *pretends* to balance "Hecate," but in reality does nothing of the kind, because of the longish "o," and because the "c" and "t" in Hecate are thin and dry, and the "lf" and "sh" of "wolfishly" are thick and soft, and therefore "wolfishly" is a longer, slower word. The soft "w" and the dim vowels, the "i" dimming from "whined" down to "wind," are meant to give the impression of a faint breeze.

In the next verse:

"In the pomp of the Mompesson house is one
Candle that looks like the midnight sun,
Or the coral comb of a cock; . . . it rocks . . .
Only the goatish snow's locks
Watch the candles lit by fright
One by one through the black night"

leaving aside the effects produced by the variations in thickness to which I have referred already, the rhythm, the drum-beating, the inevitable march onward of the menace—these are produced by the very elaborate scheme of rhymes, assonances and dissonances, "pomp," and "Mompesson" with their faint dissonances—" lolls," " coral," " cock," "rocks," " locks "—dissonances so faint they might almost be assonances, but having each its own particular thickness and depth, varying with an extraordinary subtlety. Then there are the more discordant dissonances to these, " one," " sun," and their dissonance " candle," and its shadow " black," and all these make the line heave up and down, like something struggling to escape.

In the line:

> " Or the coral comb of a cock; it rocks."

the sharp " c "s seem pin-points of light, which leap into a sudden flare with the word " comb." Later on, when we come to the lines:

> " Through the kitchen there runs a hare,
> Whinnying, whines like grass the air "

the rhythm is given by the assonances " kitchen " and " whinnying," rising to the high " i " of " whines," and by the balance of the two-syllabled, three-syllabled, and one-syllabled words; and the image was brought to my mind by the fact that thin grass trembling in the wind seems to me to resemble in its movement, a high whining or whinnying sound, whilst the dampness and coldness of the air on certain winter days, resembles the dampness and coldness of grass.

If we take the lines:

> " Black angels in a heavenly place,
> Her shady locks and her dangerous grace,"

we shall see that the rhythm is given by the high assonantal " a "s and the balance (which is completely different from that of the couplet quoted previously) of the two-syllabled, one-syllabled, and three-syllabled words.

A completely different balance, again, is given by the assonances, and the arrangement of one-syllabled, two-syllabled, and three-syllabled words in:

> " I thought I saw the wicked old witch in
> The richest gallipot in the kitchen "—

in which the sound alternately intertwines and marches forward. In:

> " a lolloping galloping candle confesses "

" lolloping " is a queer reversed dissonance of " gallipot "—" galloping " is an almost equally crazy assonance ; they convey the impression of candle-flames, blown now backwards, now sideways, and, the " l "s in these, together with the " s " sounds in " confesses " and in the lines following:

> " Outside in the passage are wildernesses
> Of darkness rustling like witches' dresses "

give the softness of the flame that is speaking; then, much later, we come to the line:

> " The mocking money in the pockets."

where the faint variations in the castanet-thin, elfish sound, seem like pin-points of candle-light, blown by the cold air.

As, earlier in the poem, we found variations in degrees of thickness, so, in:

> " Whinnying, neighed the maned blue wind."

we find variations in the degrees of thinness, and this, too, has significance.

To return to " Façade ": in the following poem the strange ghostly rhythm is formed largely by the fact that the lines end with a deliberate tunelessness, with words whose first syllable is a dissonance, whose last syllable rhymes—dissonances which, therefore, shrink as with cold, or are blown backwards and forwards as by a cold wind, changing their direction aimlessly from time to time, or gathering the rhythm together into a ghostly march-tune:

"The wind's bastinado
Whipt on the calico
Skin of the Macaroon
And the black Picaroon
Beneath the galloon
Of the midnight sky.
Came the great Soldan
In his sedan
Floating his fan—
Saw what the sly
Shadow's cocoon
In the barracoon
Held. Out they fly:
'This melon,
Sir Mammon,
Comes out of Babylon:
Buy for a patacoon,—
Sir, you must buy!'
Said Il Magnifico
Pulling a fico—
With a stoccado
And a gambado,
Making a wry
Face: 'This corraceous
Round orchidaceous
Laceous porraceous
Fruit is a lie!
It is my friend King Pharaoh's head

That nodding blew out of the Pyramid . . .'
. . . The tree's small corinths
Were hard as jacinths,
For it is winter and cold winds sigh . . .
No nightingale
In her farthingale
Of bunchèd leaves let her singing die."

In the first four lines—to examine the dissonances for a moment, "calico" shrinks after the word "bastinado,"—curls up into itself. "Picaroon" shrinks more slightly after "Macaroon," and the lines in which these dissonances occur, blow aimlessly backwards and forwards, but in the next two lines:

"Beneath the galloon
Of the midnight sky"

the rhythm is gathered together, shows a faint, not quite formulated purpose.

Throughout the poem the rhythm changes again and again, owing largely to the constant shifting of the accent from one syllable of the words ending the lines to another—from the dissonance beginning the end word, to the rhyming last syllable—and back again. When the accent shifts suddenly from the first syllable of the last word to the first word of the line, leaving the last word unaccented, as in the lines quoted below:

"This melon,
Sir Mammon,
Comes out of Babylon,
Buy for a patacoon—
Sir, you must buy!"

The change from the word "melon" to "Mammon" (so like thick dust that has gathered itself together into some embodiment), the change from the dreaminess of Babylon, which is in part a matter of association, to the sharp sound, like that of a dry coin falling on hard ground, of "patacoon," this is deliberate.

In the nine lines beginning with:

"Said Il Magnifico"

a final shaping and embodiment of the dust comes to pass. But this shaping and voicing of the dust is followed immediately by the dreaminess, in which there is no emphasis save that of the little cold air produced by the faint wavering pauses in the lines:

"It is my friend King Pharaoh's head
That nodding blew out of the Pyramid."

and their echoes (which are echoes only rhythmically, not verbally):

"For it is winter, and cold winds sigh."

. . . . . .

"Of bunchèd leaves let her singing die."

An impression of cold is obtained in the lines:

". . . The tree's small corinths
Were hard as jacinths,
For it is winter and cold winds sigh . . .
No nightingale
In her farthingale
Of bunchèd leaves let her singing die."

by the fading dissonance of "jacinths" after "corinths" and the identical ending of "nightingale," "farthingale" which sounds like something shrinking from the cold.

If we take another poem in "Façade," "The Octogenarian," we shall find that the slow and dreamy rhythm is obtained in part by the flapping to and fro of the lines, owing to the open rhyme scheme

—in part to the way in which the balance of the stress on the words ending some of the lines is reversed—changed from the unrhymed syllable, to the rhymed:—"*win*dow," "be*low*," "*night*cap," "*gap*," and by the equal balance of the two syllables of "lanthorn" coming after the heavily unequal stresses of the words ending the five previous lines:

"The octogenarian
Leaned from his window,
To the valerian
Growing below
Said: 'My nightcap
Is only the gap
In the trembling thorn
Where the mild unicorn
With the little Infanta
Danced the lavolta
(Clapping hands: molto
Lent' eleganta).'
The man with the lanthorn
Peers high and low;
No more
Than a snore
As he walks to and fro . . .
Il Dottore the stoic
Culls silver herb
Beneath the superb
Vast moon azoic."

Although the above poem is a part of the "Façade" series, the Octogenarian is an inhabitant of the countryside that we find in certain of the Bucolic Comedies, in "Fox Trot," to take one instance. This poem is an experiment in the effect on rhythm and on speed, of certain arrangements of assonances and dissonances, and of a certain arrangement of intertwining one-syllabled, two-syllabled, and three-syllabled words:

"Old
Sir
Faulk
Tall as a stork,
Before the honeyed fruits of dawn were ripe, would walk,
And stalk with a gun
The reynard-coloured sun,
Among the pheasant-feathered corn the unicorn has torn,
forlorn the
Smock-faced sheep
Sit
And
Sleep;
Periwigged as William and Mary, weep . . .
'Sally, Mary, Mattie, what's the matter, why cry?'
The huntsman and the reynard-coloured sun and I sigh:
'Oh, the nursery-maid Meg
With a leg like a peg
Chased the feathered dreams like hens, and when they laid
an egg
In the sheepskin
Meadows
Where
The serene King James would steer,
Horse and hounds, then he
From the shade of a tree
Picked it up as spoil to boil for nursery tea,' said the
mourners. In the
Corn, towers strain
Feathered tall as a crane,
And whistling down the feathered rain, old Noah goes
again—

An old dull mome
With a head like a pome,
Seeing the world as a bare egg,
Laid by the feathered air; Meg
Would beg three of these
For the nursery teas
Of Japhet, Shem, and Ham; she gave it
Underneath the trees,
Where the boiling
Water
Hissed,
Like the goose-king's feathered daughter,—kissed
Pot and pan and copper kettle
Put upon their proper mettle,
Lest the Flood—the Flood—the Flood begin again through these!"

The ground rhythm of the beginning of this poem is partly the result of the drone-sounds in the first lines, the dissonances, so subtle, they might almost be assonances, of "Faulk," "tall," "stork," "before," "walk"—each having a different depth of darkness. "Tall" and the second syllable of "before," for instance, whilst the sounds differ, though with an almost incredible faintness both in darkness and in length, dip much deeper in both cases than "Faulk," or "stork"—whilst the sound of "stork" is slightly darker than "Faulk." All these drone sounds seem pleasant country shadows, varying slightly in depth, in warmth, in length. In the fifth and seventh lines, the words "honeyed" and "reynard" are a little rounder than "pheasant feathered," and each casts a little dipping, reversed shadow, because the light fleeting character of the second syllable of "honeyed" suddenly grows dark in its dissonance, the second syllable of "reynard," whilst the first syllable of "honeyed" is a faintly darker dissonance of the "rey" of "reynard." The shadows, therefore, fall in opposite directions.

The fact that in the line:

> "The reynard-coloured sun"

the words ending in "d" are placed so close together, makes a slight leap into the air, while, some lines further on, the three-syllabled words of:

> "Periwigged as William and Mary, weep"

twirl round on themselves; and the assonances, placed in such close juxtaposition, of:

> "Among the pheasant-feathered corn, the
> unicorn has torn, forlorn the"

give an extraordinary smoothness; the lines might consist of one word only were it not for the change from sunniness to darkness.

The "ea" sounds on which much of the poem is based, vary in lightness; at moments the effect is of light pleasant stretches of corn-fields, as in:

> "Among the pheasant-feathered corn the unicorn has torn,
> forlorn the," etc.

over which the flying shadows of the darker vowelled "corn," "unicorn," "torn," "forlorn," dip and are gone. Sometimes, the effect is of a duller, block-headed, rustic indifference, as in:

> "Oh the nursery-maid Meg
> With a leg like a peg,"

Whilst at other times we have a thicker, plumaged sound, which is not the result of association alone, as in:

"Chased the *fea*thered dreams like h*ens*, and wh*en* they
laid an egg
In the sheepskin
*Mea*dows
Where."

In the line:

"Sally, Mary, Mattie, what's the matter, why cry?"

the changing of the assonances, from the limpness of "Sally" to the hardness of "Mattie," the reversal of sound in the second syllables, from "Mattie" to "matter"—these have a very faint effect upon the rhythm, whilst the exact rhymes "Why cry" placed together, give a high leap into the air. Throughout the poem, the assonances and dissonances are placed in a closely concerted and interwoven design, some being accented, and some so unaccented as to be almost muted; they are largely responsible for the rhythm, and often counterpoint it slightly, as in:

"Oh the nursery-*maid* Meg
With a leg like a peg
Chased the feathered dreams like hens, and when *they laid*
an egg"

where the high "a" sounds counterpoint the "Meg," "leg," "peg," "egg," sound of the ground rhythm.

These "a" (or ai) sounds, are echoed further on, more insistently, and with a deeper emphasis, by

". . . In the
Corn, towers *strain*
Feathered tall as a *crane*,
And whistling down the feathered *rain*, old Noah goes
again"—

where these assonances, whilst they are slightly

counterpointed, are yet nearly as important as the ground-rhythm given by " corn " and " tall."

It will be seen how slack is the rhythm, in comparison with the rest, of such lines as have only an end rhyme, and no apparent assonances or dissonances, as in the second line of:

> " An old dull mome
> With a head like a pome."

Though " head " is immediately linked up again in the next line with " egg," yet, because it had no previous related sound, there is no effect on rhythm.

A faint and fleeting country shadow is cast again, later in the poem, by the changing of the " aph " of " Japhet " to the dimmer " v " of " gave " in the lines:

> " Of Japhet, Shem, and Ham, she gave it
> Underneath the trees."

But all these experiments were, more or less, a preparation for the poem called " Gold Coast Customs," and of this I can only write from a technical point of view; it was written with anguish, and I would not willingly re-live that birth. I will therefore confine myself to mentioning certain technical details.

The organization of the poem, of a world where all the natural rhythms of the spirit, of the soil, and of the seasons, have broken down, but where a feverish intertwining seething movement, a vain seeking for excitement, still exists, presented considerable difficulty. I have tried to give a concentrated essence of the present age, through a movement, which at times interweaves like worms intertwining, which at times has a jaunty wire-jerked sound, or rears itself up like a tidal wave rushing forward, or swells like a black sea-swell by means of violently-stretching vowels, then, as in lines:

> " Hidden behind
> The Worm's mask grown
> White as a bone
> Where eyeholes rot wide
> And are painted for sight "

sinks into a deliberate pulselessness. In this world of the "rich man Judas, brother Cain," and of that world's confession, Lady Bamburgher, man is part ravenous beast of prey, part worm, part ape, or is but the worm turned vertebrate. It is a world where the light is no longer a reality, but a high ventriloquist sound (so high none knows whence it comes), the octave of the black clotted night—no longer the true and guiltless Light:

> " (Christ that takest away the sin
> Of the world, and the rich man's bone-dead grin) "

This is all I can bring myself to say about the poem, excepting from a technical point of view.

Down to the end of the second verse of the second page, the poem is obviously nothing but abstract sound—abstract, but I would like to think significant. In the first verse, the rocking drum-beating movement is produced by the various flatnesses and depths of the " a "s, the thicknesses and dullnesses of the " u "s, and by the intertwining of words of different lengths (since these produce different speeds). In the first four lines:

> " One fantee wave
> Is grave and tall
> As brave Ashantee's
> Thick mud wall."

the first line begins with a jaunty wire-jerked movement. From the fawning, crouching sound of "fainter" it rises suddenly (stretching outward), with "wave," to one of the utmost heights of which a vowel-sound is capable—echoed by "grave" in the next line, which rocks up and down between that enormous height and the deepest darkness, with the hollow sound of "tall." The first line is echoed, but upside down, in the third. By this means the lines toss up and down violently, from a world-height down into the deepest gulf imaginable, and this tossing up and down is repeated in the third verse:

> " Like monkey-skin
> In the sea—one sin
> Like a weasel is nailed to bleach on the rocks
> Where the eyeless mud screeched fawning, mocks " . . .

by means of the high screaming "e"s alternating with dulled "o"s, while the arrangement of soft "s"s, and of their slightly firmer counterpart the "ch"s, give a feeling of gradually rotting flesh.

In the following verse:

> " At a negro that wipes
> His knife . . . dug there
> A bugbear bellowing
> Bone dared rear—
> A bugbear bone that bellows white
> As the ventriloquist sound of light."

we find the most giddy rocking sound that has yet been produced in this poem—and this is the result of the rhymes "dug there," "bugbear," being placed so close together, followed by the deafening blows of the alliterative "b"s, with gaps between, numb like deafness, where a continued alliteration is expected and is not found. (*Note.* In " Fox Trot," two rhymes placed close together " Why cry " " I sigh " produced a leap into the air; but the result of " dug there," " bugbear " is entirely different, because " there " and " bear " are words of faintly more than one syllable, and because " dug " and " bug " are low sounds, and " there " and " bear " are both higher and stretch forward, instead of crouching.)

The long echoing hollowness of:

> " A bugbear bellowing
> Bone dared rear—
> A bugbear bone that bellows white "

actually lengthens and slows the lines, the first two being stretched violently and to their uttermost capacity.

The verse about a slum, which begins with the line:

> " Here, tier on tier,"

gives a suggestion of flapping emptiness, because of the word " tier " having more than one syllable.

Certain images in the poem were taken from objects seen in the Ethnographical section of the British Museum—the shrunken heads, for instance, and that image in which the sun:

> " . . . hangs like a skull
> With a yellow dull
> Face made of clay
> (Where tainted, painted, the plague-spots bray)
> To hide where the real face rotted away."

Here, though in quite a different sense, with a different sound, than that of a previous verse, we have again—resulting this time from the dull crumbling " l "s,—

the sense of flesh decaying. But in this verse, we have a hopeless endeavour to rise, produced this time by using poignant vowels alternating with thick muddy ones; but this endeavour, in lines 7, 8 and 9 of the verse in question, becomes mere hallucination and fever. With the succeeding verse, when we come to the lines:

> " Of the shapeless worm-soft unshaping Sin—
> Unshaping till no more the beat of the blood
> Can raise up the body from endless mud "

the position of the " a "s and "s "s in the first line gives an impression of formlessness endeavouring (in the second and third lines) to regain shape by means of the alliterative " b "s. There should, however, to attain this aim, have been a third " b " where the word " no " stands—(the omission was deliberate)—and the formless matter sinks back once more, therefore, into the mud and slime, in the line:

> " Are painted upon each unshaped form "

where the position of the " a "s produces this impression of formlessness, because they were put, deliberately, in the wrong place. And the formlessness is not that of primeval matter, it is that of matter which has chosen to be part of the slime and mud. The lines have purposely an unpleasant softness—the softness of corruption.

Throughout the poem, my method of producing the different degrees of darkness has been that of using changing wave-lengths of vowels, as in the description of Lady Bamburgher's unborn god who:

> " . . . still has bones to rot:
> A bloodless and an unborn thing"

But this deadness changes suddenly to the piteous stirring, the upheaval caused by the internal rhymes, the upward-heaving vowels, sinking and heaving upward again, of:

> " That cannot wake, yet cannot sleep,
> That makes no sound, that cannot weep,
> That hears all, bears all, cannot move—
> It is buried so deep
> Like a shameful thing
> In that plague-spot heart, Death's last dust-heap."

Much earlier in the poem, in the lines:

> " Where flaps degraded
> The black and sated
> Slack macerated
> And antiquated
> Beckoning negress
> Nun of the shade."

the degrees of the mud are given by the " s "s, by the softening of the sound of " degraded " to that of " sated," and by the change from the squelching sound of the " qu " in " antiquated," to the still softer sound of " shade."

In the succeeding verse:

> " And the rickety houses
> Rock and rot,
> Lady Bamburgher airs
> That foul plague-spot
> Her romantic heart.
> From the cannibal mart,
> That smart Plague-cart
> Lady Bamburgher rolls where the foul news-sheet
> And the shambles for souls are set in the street;"

" Rock " is a shrunken, darker echo of " rickety,"

" rot " is a still deader flatter echo of " rock," whilst the dissonance of " plague-spot," and " heart " are deliberate. The arrangement of " l "s placed near each other, gives the effect of a stretch of mud, clinging to our feet and impeding our progress. Later in the same verse we return to the rocking movement, tossing up and down, which is effected by the internal rhymes and dissonances.

Much later in the poem when we come to the verse:

> " In the sailor's tall
> Ventriloquist street
> The calico dummies
> Flap and meet;
> Calculate: ' Sally go
> Pick up a sailor.'
> Behind that façade
> The worm is a jailer."

the worm-twisting movement, the horrible softness, is produced in part by the half-rhymes—some broken or crumbled—some scarcely rhymes at all, but assonances—" calico," " calculate," " Sally go,"—in part by the soft " l "s and the dull lifeless " a "s. And four verses on, in

> " Once I saw it come
> Through the canvas slum,
> Rattle and beat what seemed a drum,
> Rattle and beat it with a bone.
> O Christ, that bone was dead, alone!
> Christ, Who will speak to such ragged Dead
> As me, I am dead, alone and bare,
> They expose me still to the grinning air,
> I shall never gather my bones and my dust
> Together (so changed and scattered, lost . . .)
> So I can be decently burièd.

What is that whimpering like a child
That this mad ghost beats like a drum in the air?
The heart of Sal
That once was a girl
And now is a calico thing to loll
Over the easy steps of the slum
Waiting for something dead to come."

the language has produced all the effect, with the horrible thick deadness of the sound of "slum" and "drum"; whilst the deliberate tuneless soft deadness of the dissonances "Sal," "girl," "loll" seem toppling down hill into some thick abyss.

Throughout the whole poem, I have tried to produce, not so much the record of a world, as the wounded and suffering soul of that world, its living evocation, not its history, seen through the eyes of a protagonist whose personal tragedy is echoed in that vaster tragedy. Of the other implicit meanings of the poem, I am unwilling to speak.

THE SLEEPING BEAUTY

To Osbert

I

When we come to that dark house,
Never sound of wave shall rouse
The bird that sings within the blood
Of those who sleep in that deep wood:
For in that house the shadows now
Seem cast by some dark unknown bough.
The gardener plays his old bagpipe
To make the melons' gold seeds ripe;
The music swoons with a sad sound—
" Keep, my lad, to the good safe ground!
For once, long since, there was a felon
With guineas gold as the seeds of a melon,
And he would sail for a far strand
To seek a waking, clearer land,—
A land whose name is only heard
In the strange singing of a bird.
The sea was sharper than green grass,
The sailors would not let him pass,
For the sea was wroth and rose at him
Like the turreted walls of Jerusalem,
Or like the towers and gables seen
Within a deep-boughed garden green.

And the sailors bound and threw him down
Among those wrathful towers to drown.
And oh, far best," the gardener said,
" Like fruits to lie in your kind bed,—
To sleep as snug as in the grave
In your kind bed, and shun the wave,
Nor ever sigh for a strange land
And songs no heart can understand."

I hunted with the country gentlemen
Who, seeing Psyche fly, thought her a hen

And aimed at her ; the mocking wingèd one
Laughed at their wingless state, their crooked gun.

Then on the water—green and jewelled leaves
Hiding ripe fruitage—every sportsman grieves,

Sitting and grumbling in their flat boat edged
With the soft feathers of the foam, scarce fledged.

But I will seek again the palace in the wood,
Where never bird shall rouse our sleepy blood

Within the bear-dark forests, far beyond
This hopeless hunting, or Time's sleepy bond.

. . . . .

The gardener was old as tongues of nightingales,
That in the wide leaves tell a thousand Grecian tales

And sleep in golden nets of summer light.
" Sweet fig," he called me, and would stay the flight

Of plums that seemed Jove's golden-feathered rain.
Then, birds like Fortunatus moved again

Among the boughs with silent feathered feet,—
Spraying down dew like jewels amid the sweet

Green darkness; figs, each like a purse of gold,
Grow among leaves like rippled water green, and cold.

" Beneath those laden boughs," the gardener sighs,
" Dreaming in endlessness, forgotten beauty lies.

Long since, a wandering and airy nymph
She seemed, when the bright ladies of the court
Came like the sylvan equipage Dian
Leads in her hunting through the deepest woods
And the Dodonian leaves of summer; only now
We see them smile, an echo through dim leaves."

Thus spoke the ancient man, wrinkled like old moon-
light
Beneath dark boughs. Time dreamed away to night,
And while I heard the leaves like silver cymbals ring
He told me this old tale of Beauty's mournful
christening:—

Oh the pomp that passed those doors;
Trains still sweep the empty floors,
Pelongs, bulchauls, pallampores,

Soundless now as any breeze,
Of amber and of orangeries
That sweep from isles in Indian seas;

While in the floating and mysterious leaves
A silver sound like some forgotten music grieves.

The fairies all received an invitation,
Ordered their sedan-chairs with great elation,

Their richest trains, their plumes, and their bright
trumps,
Like silver fruits that from dark branches grow in
clumps.

The fays descend from each dark palanquin
With fanfares and with lute sounds, walk within

The shade ; there, smiling dim as satyr-broods
Hornèd as moons, that haunt our deepest woods,

Are country gentlemen, so countrified
That in their rustic grace they try to hide

Their fingers sprouting into leaves ; we see
Them sweet as cherries growing from a tree—

All fire and snow ; they grow and never move,
Each in the grace of his Pan-haunted grove.

" Her mouth," the first fay said, " as fair shall be
As any gentle ripe red strawberry

That grows among the thickest silver leaves ;
Her locks shall be as blonde as these—the eve's

Great winds of beauty, fleeces from those flocks
That Dian tends in her deep woods, those locks

Shall seem." The second fairy said,
" Blessings like dew fall on her lovely head!

For lovely as the cherubim's soft breath,
Or Leda's love, whose cold melodious death

Is heavenly music to the sad world lost,
Her skin shall be, as fair as silver frost."

But now within the dark shade of a deep-dreaming
    tree
A darker shade and panoply we see,

Drowning the soft sound of the plashing lute,
A great fanfare is heard, like unripe silver fruit.

" Who is this now who comes? " Dark words reply
    and swoon
Through all the high cold arbours of the moon:

" The slighted Laidronette, the unbidden fay,
Princess of the Pagodas. . . . Shades, make way! "

The sedan-chair that hides her shade is mellow
As the trees' great fruit-jewels glittering yellow,

And round it the old turbanned ladies flock
Like apes that try to pluck an apricock.

The little fawning airs are trembling wan;
And silver as fair Leda's love, the swan,

The moonlight seems; the apricocks have turned to
amber,
Cold as from the bright nymph Thetis' chamber,

And far away, the fountains sigh forlorn
As waving rustling sheaves of silver corn.

The wicked fay descended, mopping, mowing
In her wide-hooped petticoat, her water-flowing

Brightly-perfumed silks. . . . " Ah, ha, I see
You have remembered all the fays but me! "

(She whipped her panthers, golden as the shade
Of afternoon in some deep forest glade.)

" I am very cross because I am old,
And my tales are told,
And my flames jewel-cold.

I will make your bright birds scream,
I will darken your jewelled dream,
I will spoil your thickest cream.

I will turn the cream sour,
I will darken the bower,
I will look through the darkest shadows and lour,—

And sleep as dark as the shade of a tree
Shall cover you . . . Don't answer me!
For if the Princess prick her finger
Upon a spindle, then she shall be lost

As a child wandering in a glade of thorn,
With sleep like roses blowing soft, forlorn,
Upon each bough. This, madam, is the cost
Of your dark rudeness. But I will not linger."

And with a dark dream's pomp and panoply
She swept out with her train; the soft sounds die,
Of plumaged revelry bright as her train
Of courtiers; and all was night again.

Then through the deepest shades went Laidronette,
Princess of the Pagodas; in a pet
She left the domes, like rich and turbanned fruits
In the great gardens, and she left the lutes;

Back to her palace in her great sedan
She floats; worlds turn to snow before her fan.
She sweeps through the dark woods to her vast palace
Where now, at last, she can unleash her malice.

There in her room, an amber orange burned
On the Hesperides' dark trees and spurned
By that gold-peruked conqueror the Sun—
(An Alexander whence plumed rivers run,

Fearing his fierceness,) Ethiopian shapes
The heat had kissed, with lips like burning grapes,
Unwigged her for the night, while her apes beg
That she will leave uncurtained that Roc's egg,

Her head, a mount of diamonds bald and big
In the ostrich feathers that compose her wig.
Her dwarfs as round as oranges of amber
Among the tall trees of the shadow clamber,

And in Night's deep domain she monstrous lies
With every little wicked dream that flies
And crawls; with old Bacchantes black with wine,
Whose very hair has changed into a vine,

And ancient satyrs whose wry wig of roses
Nothing but little rotting shames discloses;
They lie where shadows, cold as the night breeze,
Seem cast by rocks, and never by kind trees.

II

NEXT dawn, the ancient chamberlain
Came like someone who has lain

For years beneath the deepest water. . . .
He called the housekeeper's young daughter,

Where she sat in her bedgown,
Smoothing the dusky dawn's owl-down,

Until she leaned out through the wet
Leaves in her pale sarsanet:

" Forget the dawn is still owl-dark,
Forget the wet leaves . . . you must hark:

Owing to the fairy's malice,
No spindles must be in the palace."

In their dark leaf-hid bower the maidens chatter like a
    bird
Awakening: " Phœbe, Audrey, have you heard?

Oh, the dark panic here this very night,
The slighted fairy's anger and our good queen's fright,

And all our spindles banished! it would seem
That we have naught to do all day but dream!"

When the dew seems like trembling silver leaves,
Cross Poll Troy looks out through the palace eaves....

"Knot up your butter-yellow satin hair,
You lazy queans. ... Come quick! come down the
stair!

Anne, Anne,
Come draw the milk!
The cream must be as thick as silk
And yellow as the ripest sheen
Of apricock or nectarine.
Beneath the great leaves of that tree
Wicked Goat-foot I can see!
He'll steal the milk and steal the cream
While you lie in a lazy dream.
Fie, the lazy birds, the shames!
Phœbe, you must light the flames;
They will spring like greenest leaves
Growing round your bower's dim eaves.
Oh the foliage shrill and green
In the fire! you lazy quean,
Dream not of your heart's desire,—
Phœbe, come and light the fire!"

III

THEN through the broad green leaves the gardener
came
With a basket filled with honeyed fruits of dawn
Plucked from the thickest leaves. They heard him
sing
As he walked where that pillared avenue
Of tall clear-fruited ripe trees grew
(For so the Palace seemed); and sweet
His song fled, soft as wind and fleet:

" Now the dawn lights seem
Ripe yellow fruits in a dream
Among the great green leaves
Of dawn and rustling sheaves.

The vast sun's rays like sheaves of wheat
Are gold and dry,
All bound together, growing yet—
An early offering. I

Heard the old King's lullabies
That his nurse the South Wind sighs,
As she heaps the honeycombs
Where he lies; the fruit-ripe domes

All around him, clear and sweet. . . .
And now the old King's cockscomb crown
Is nodding, falls a-down, a-down. . . .
Till the golden sheaves of the sun shall be mown
He will lie in the palace above the wheat.

The dew all tastes of ripening leaves;
Dawn's tendril fingers heap
The yellow honeyed fruits whose clear
Sound flows into his sleep.

Those yellow fruits and honeycomb. . . .
' Lulla-lullaby,'
Shrilled the dew on the broad leaves—
' Time itself must die—
(—must die ').

Now in the palace the maidens knead
And bake the little loaves of the bread,
Gold as the sun; they sighing said,
' When will the sun begin to seed
And waken the old Dead ?—
(cold Dead) ? ' "

IV

Do, do,
Princess, do,
The fairy Chatte Blanche rocks you slow.
Like baskets of white fruit or pearls
Are the fairy's tumbling curls,—
Or lattices of roses white
Wherethrough the snows like doves take flight.
Do, do,
Princess, do,
How furred and white is the fallen snow.

Do, do,
Princess, do,
Like singing blackbirds are the eyes
Of the fairy old and wise.
A honeyed tune, the crystal drops
Of rain that falls, and never stops,
From flowers as white as seraphims'
Breath no winter ever dims. . . .
Do, do,
Princess, do,
Like birds that peck fruit sweet and shrill
With painted bill,
Flies down the snow.

The angels came with footsteps light,
They brushed her hair to make it bright,
They taught her to be sweet and wise
With kisses faint as butterflies.

They said, " When you go up to heaven
The nursery clock shall ne'er strike seven.
Your boudoir shall be of white satin,
You shall not say your prayers in Latin—
But you shall dance a minuet
On heaven's floors; frizzed mignonette
Shall seem your curls, of heaven's flowers
Most fair; and you shall sit in bowers

Of honeysuckle sweet as those pink fires
Whereby the angels dry their locks upon the light's
gold wires."

And when the Queen called for her child, they brought
Only her image, formed to please the Court. . . .

An old man with a gardener's hat and red
Poll-parrot nose brought her a tiny bed

Whereon lies folded a small poppet rose
That in her dark leaves like a little babe lies close.

For after Laidronette's wild rage was spent,
The chamberlain to the child's nursery went

And sped her far away, like the East Wind,
To worlds of snow, far from the fairy's mind.

And there the Princess stayed till she was weaned
From milk of doves; then o'er the snow, bright-
preened.

By its sharp bill, the wind, the chamberlain
Whisked the Princess back to the Court again.

V

But the Dowager Queen shook her old head:
" The rose, the peach, and the quince-flower red
And the strawberry flower in the snows are dead.
If none of the rose-tribe can survive
The snow, then how can our poppet live? "

And in her gown of quilted satin,
As red as quince-flowers, she reads Latin
Missals to the peaches that grow
Gilded with suns, then fade like snow;

They lie in the nets of dew at leisure.
And this is now her only pleasure—
This and her parrot long ago
Dead,—but none dared tell her so,

And therefore the bird was stuffed and restored
To lifeless immortality; bored
It seemed, but yet it remained her own;
And she never knew the bird's soul had flown.

And so indeed seemed Destiny,—
A bird fine-feathered, fair to see
In spite of its condor-wings, fierce beak,
And hooded eyes. . . . Grown old and weak,

Imprisoned now in a gilded cage
In her powder-closet, far from the rage
Of winter, it can only sing
Roulades, and preen its bright clipped wing

Upon her perfumed dressing table
In a cage with a foolish bell-hung gable,
Beneath the portrait of dead Queen Anne
(Whose life was the sweet air blown from a fan),

'Midst brightly perfumed water-flowing
Eighteenth-century silks where growing
Strawberry flowers of the frail frost
Upon the diamond-panes are lost.

VI

At Easter when red lacquer buds sound far slow
Quarter-tones for the old dead Mikado,

Through avenues of lime trees, where the wind
Sounds like a chapeau chinois, shrill, unkind,—

The Dowager Queen, a curling Korin wave
That flows for ever past a coral cave,

With Dido, Queen of Carthage, slowly drives
(Her griffin dog that has a thousand lives)

Upon the flat-pearled and fantastic shore
Where curled and turbanned waves sigh "Never
more."

And she is sunk beneath a clear still lake
Of sleep,—so frail with age she cannot wake. . . .

A strange horizon and a soundless sea
Must separate wise age from you and me—

They watch life's movements ripening like fruit
And sigh, knowing the gnarled and twisted root.

O people building castles on the sand,
And taking one another by the hand,

What do you find within each other's eyes?—
What wisdom unknown of the lonely wise?—

The promise of what spring, the certainty
Of what eternal life to come,—what lie?

Only the sound of Time's small muffled drum,
The sound of footsteps that will never come,

And little marches all beribboned gay
That lead down the lime avenues away

To the dark grave . . . we for a little weep,
Then pray a little, sinking into sleep.

How far is this wise age from the bright youth
Of Princess Cydalise, a warm wind from the south?

VII

In the great nursery where the poppet maids
Seem small round fruits that grow in leafy glades,

The Princess grew in beauty still she seemed
That gentle maid of whom Endymion dreamed.

And in those evenings when the lovely moon
Shone through the smiling woods of deepest June,

Then through the curtains she would play " Bo-Peep "
With fleecy lamb-tailed clouds, when she should sleep.

Sometimes the moon would sing her ancient songs
Of lovely ladies and forgotten wrongs;

And once she whispered that within the wood
An ancient satyr, wiser than the brood

From which he sprang, within a cloudy cave
Teaches philosophies both old and grave.

The Princess said, " With my light step I will be gone,
To peep within that far cave—but alone! "

Yet in the darkness, her gazelle-light footsteps ran
Far from the cave of that wise satyr-man.

VIII

In the great gardens, after bright spring rain,
We find sweet innocence come once again,
White periwinkles, little pensionnaires
With muslin gowns and shy and candid airs,

That under saint-blue skies, with gold stars sown,
Hide their sweet innocence by spring winds blown,
From zephyr libertines that like Richelieu
And d'Orsay their gold-spangled kisses blew;

And lilies of the valley whose buds blonde and tight
Seem curls of little school-children that light
The priests' procession, when on some saint's day
Along the country paths they make their way;

Forget-me-nots, whose eyes of childish blue,
Gold-starred like heaven, speak of love still true;
And all the flowers that we call " dear heart,"
Who say their prayers like children, then depart

Into the dark. Amid the dew's bright beams
The summer airs, like Weber waltzes, fall
Round the first rose who flushed with her youth seems
Like young Princesses dressed for their first ball:

Who knows what beauty ripens from dark mould
After the sad wind and the winter's cold?—
But a small wind sighed, colder than the rose
Blooming in desolation, " No one knows."

IX

The Princess was young as the innocent flowers
That bloom and love through the bright spring hours;
Sometimes she crept through locked doors to annoy
The palace housekeeper, cross Mrs. Troy,
Who kept all the whimpering sad ghosts locked
In a cupboard, was grieved and faintly shocked
If the Princess Jehanne, long since dead,
Whose hair was of costly long gold thread,
Would slip her flat body, like a gleaming
Quivering fish in a clear pool dreaming,
Through the deep mesh of a conversation,
Making some ghostly imputation;—
Or if she frightened the maids till they wince
By stealing a withered gold-crowned quince
Wherewith they make preserves; in the gloom
She seems, as she glimmers round the room,
Like a lovely milk-white unicorn
In a forestial thicket of thorn.

Life was so still, so clear, that to wake
Under a kingfisher's limpid lake
In the lovely afternoon of a dream
Would not remote or stranger seem.
Everything seemed so clear for a while—
The turn of a head or a deep-seen smile;
Then a smile seen through wide leaves or deep water,
That beauty seemed to the King's daughter;
For a flying shadow passed, then gone
Was the gleam, and the Princess was alone.

How sweet seemed the flowers of spring again—
As pink as Susan and Polly and Jane,
Like country maids so sweet and shy
Who bloom and love and wonder not why:
Now when summer comes it seems the door
To the graves that lie under the trivial floor,
And the gardens hard to touch and shining,
Where no mirage dew lies whining.
And the sweet flowers seem for a fading while
Dear as our first love's youthful smile,—
Till they bruise and wound the heart and sense
With their lost and terrible innocence.

X

When each clear raindrop holds for flight
A wingless world all plumage-bright,

Like crystal-clear wysteria,
After the storm's hysteria,

The Princess visited the farm
Where all the beasts lie, furred as palm

That on the budding Easter boughs
Among the winds of beauty grows.

The farm-pond, fruitish-soft and ripe,
Was smooth as a daguerreotype;

The farm-maid, Rosa, under flimsy
Muslin skies, an angel's whimsy,

Walked. . . . Her daisy-frillèd frock
Was stiff and harder than a rock,

Frills touch her feet, like plants foam down;
Her wooden trellised hair is brown.

The grass is furry as a bear
With heat; the donkey's panniers flare

With fruits whose clear complexions, waxen,
Hide in leaves all hairy-flaxen.

And from the sky, white angels lean
To stroke poor Dobbin's palm-furred skin,

And pluck from the round leaves the pink
Schoolgirlish summer fruits that wink—

Giggle insipidly. On winding
Roads whose dust seems gilded binding

Made for " Paul et Virginie "—
(So flimsy-tough those roads are), see

The panniered donkey pass ! The ass's
Thoughts as through the dust he passes

Where leaves seem parasols of gauze
Shading the striped wooden floors,

Seem like this : " When long ago
I worked for Balaam, never so

Appeared an angel! times are stranger
Now," and turning to his manger

He longs, for loads have made him weary,
For gentian stars, all rough and hairy,

And trees that bear white satin streamers
Of lovely flowers to please poor dreamers.

The Princess passed goats, gold as wheat,
With a kind white milky bleat,

Under the wide leaves mild as milk;
The billowing pigs with ears of silk;

Maternal cows with a white horn
As hard and dry as rustling corn—

All the poor shadows cast by our sad earthly dress
Of faults and virtues, wavering childishness!

XI

When we were young, how beautiful life seemed!—
The boundless bright horizons that we dreamed,

And the immortal music of the Day and Night,
Leaving the echo of their wonder and their might

Deep in our hearts and minds. How could the dust
Of superstitions taught in schoolrooms, lust

In love's shape, dim our beauty? What dark lie,
Or cruelty's voice, could drown this God-made
harmony?

For we knew naught of prison-worlds man built
Around us that we may not know man's guilt,—

The endless vistas of the goatish faces
Echoing each other, and the basis

Of clay, the plumeless wings of Destiny,
The vistas leading only to the grave where we must lie.

. . . . .

Then all the beauty of the world lay deep
Mirrored within the beauty water-clear
Of flowering boughs; Helen and Deirdre dreamed
And fading, wakened in that loveliness
Of watery branches. In that dead wild spring
Through the bird's shaken voice we heard God sing.

But age has dimmed our innocent paradise
With a faint shadow, shaken dust within our eyes,—
And we are one now with the lonely wise,
Knowing the spring is only the clear mirage
Of an eternal beauty that is not.
Those were the days when the fleet summer seemed
The warmth and infinite loveliness of God,
Who cared for us, within a childish heaven.
We could believe then! Oh the lips and eyes
That spoke of some far undimmed paradise!
Those were the days. . . .

XII

Now that the summer only seems the sad
Mechanical dull action of the light
And shadow playing over a dead world—
Dead as my heart—it seems too long ago
For the remembrance of the beauty and the world we
used to know;

When the warm lights of afternoon were mellow
As honeyed yellow pears, the Princess played
At Troy Town in the palace garden, tossed
And through the smiling leaves of summer lost
A round compact gold ball, the smaller image
Of this hard world, grown dry of any love—
Or walked upon the shore, watched the fantastic
Arabesque, the horsemanship of waves.
" Mademoiselle Fantoche, where do they go ? "
A faint cold wind replied, " I do not know."

THE PRINCESS

" Upon the infinite shore by the sea
The lovely ladies are walking like birds,
Their gowns have the beauty, the feathery
Grace of a bird's soft raiment; remote
Is their grace and their distinction,—they float
And peck at their deep and honeyed words
As though they were honeyed fruits; and this
Is ever their life, between sleep and bliss.
Though they are winged for enchanted flight,
They yet remain ever upon the shore
Of Eternity, seeking for nothing more,
Until the cold airs dull their beauty
And the snows of winter load those dazzling
Wings, and no bird-throat can sing! "

THE GOVERNANTE

" Look not on the infinite wave,
Dream not of the siren cave,
Nor hear the cold wind in the tree
Sigh of worlds we cannot see.

(*She sings*)
The hot muscatelle
Siesta time fell,
And the Spanish belle
Looked out through her shutters.

Under the eglantine
Thorny and lean
A shadow was playing a mandoline, mutters

Only this: ' Wave
Your fan . . . siren cave
Never was cold as the wind from the grave.'

The governante
Came walking andante,—
Sailed like a brigantine, black of brow.

And the falconette
Who danced a ballette
Sang on the pretty, the brunette bough :

' The ambassade
Of shadows invade
Death's most ultimate, peaceful shade. . . .
Lovely lady, where are you now? '

. . . . .

Come, Madam, you must eat your creamy curd,
Soft as the plumage of a bird,—

Break through the jewelled branches' bird-soft gloom
And find Malinn within the cool still-room."

XIII

WHERE reynard-haired Malinn
Walks by rock and cave,
The Sun, a Chinese mandarin,
Came dripping from the wave.

"Your hair seems like the sunrise
O'er Persia and Cathay—
A rose-red music strange and dim
As th' embalmèd smile of seraphim,"

He said to her by the white wave
In the water-pallid day;
(A forest of white coral boughs
Seemed the delicate sea-spray):

"In envy of your brighter hair,—
Since, Madam, we must quarrel,—
I've changed the cold flower-lovely spray
To branches of white coral;

And when, white muslin madam, you
Coquette with the bright wind,
I shall be but thin rose-dust;
He will be cold, unkind."

The flowers that bud like rain and dream
On thin boughs water-clear,
Fade away like a lovely music
Nobody will hear,

And Eolus and Boreas
Brood among those boughs,
Like hermits haunting the dark caves
None but the wise man knows.

But Malinn's reynard-coloured hair,
Amid the world grown sere

Still seemed the Javanese sunrise
Whose wandering music will surprise
Into cold bird-chattering cries
The Emperor of China
Lying on his bier.

XIV

The birds, strange flashing glints of another life,
Peck at the fruits of summer, that too soon
Will fade into a little gilded dust.
Then underneath the dancing, glancing bough
Came Malinn, with her round cheeks dyed as pink
As the insipid empty-tasting fruits
Of summer giggling through the rounded leaves.

Outside the stillroom was a cherry tree,
And through the dancing shadows she could see
Cross ancient Poll Troy come to do her duty. . . .
She had a cold frost-bitten beauty
Like blue moonlight smooth and cold
As amber; with her trembling old
Hands she tied the boughs aloft
Through the air all creamy soft;
Then on the sill of the woodland dairy,
Moving as quick and light as a fairy,
She put a bowl of the thickest cream
(As thick as chestnut flowers in a dream).
The gossiping naiad of the water,
In her sprigged gown like the housekeeper's daughter,
Giggles outside the stillroom; she
Plucks at the thick-bustled cherry tree.

And Poll is cross; she chases cherried
Country maids like thickest-berried
Cherry trees in their ruched gown
Till they run from the palace, down,
Like the sprigged muslin waterfalls
Of this clear country, to where calls
Pan, with his satyrs on the rocks
Feeding their wave-weary flocks.
The naiad's giggling irritates
Cross Poll Troy till at last she rates
Her through the thick-leaved cherry tree:
" My eyes are dim,—I yet can see
You, lazy quean! Go work!" "I can't."
" I say you shall!" " I say I shan't!"
" But when the airs are creamy soft
And candle-flames are quince flowers, oft
Though my heart flutters like a bird,
All dream-dark, though as soft as curd
The moonlight seems still, from my bed
I rise and work, you sleepy head!
Though I am dim and very old,
I wake the flames all jewel-cold,
The flames that seem, when they soar high,
Like waterfalls of jewels; you sigh,
While I, Miss, churn and make the curd,"
Piped Poll Troy like a small cross bird,
Then shuts the stillroom window, goes, for she
Still hears the naiad giggling through the tree.

But Malinn stays where the deep fire's red flowers
Should be as sweet and red as hawthorn bowers.

(*She sings*)
" The purring fire has a bear's dull fur,
Its warmth is sticky, dark as a burr. . . .
Come drowse, for now there is no eye
To watch, no voice to ask me why!
All night I hear my animal blood
Cry to my youth, ' Come to the wood ' . . .
But Darkness lumbers like a bear,
Grumbling, cumbers floor and stair. . . .
And on the eightieth step, I know
That on the moon's green lichen stain
I'll slip . . . and his dark breath will blow
My light out . . . . All will be still again! "

She cried out to the naiad: " I have torn
My flimsy dress upon a thicket's thorn;
The petal of a briar-rose lies forlorn
Upon it." Through the glinting leaves about the dairy
Appeared the cream-smug face of the wicked fairy. . . .
" You've torn your dress, my poppet. . . . I'll come
in. . . .
I've brought my spindle with me and I'll spin
A dress for you. . . .
Such grey-blue sleeves!
Of muslin, like the wind of eve's!
It shall have frills that flare like leaves;

The ribbons shall be preened,
Quilled prettily and sheened
As when the courtier-wind plays with a flock
Of birds for battledore and shuttlecock—
Whose feathers stream like ribbons. I will hide
A jewel within each one: you'll seem a bride

For Ariel or some rich water-god. . . . Come, spin! "
Malinn looked through the leaves. . . . " Ma'am,
please come in! "

Far off, the Martha-coloured scabious
Grew among dust as dry as old Eusebius,

And underneath the cotton-nightcap trees
Wanders a little cold pig-snouted breeze.

Then in a gown all filled with foliage like hell's fires,
And quilled like nests of cockatrices, with the light's
gold wires

Sewing it stiff, old Laidronette the fairy
Crept through the window of the woodland dairy.

Butter and cream
Turn hard as a jewel,
The shrill flames scream,
The leaves mutter " cruel."

Through the dark jewelled leaves
See the Princess peep
As lovely as eve's
Soft wind of sleep.

She picks up the spindle. " Oh, the curious
bliss! . . .
. . . It pricks my finger now. How strange this is,—
For I am like that lovely fawn-queen dead
Long since,—pierced through the pool-clear heart,"
she said.

Her room now seems like some pale cave
Haunted by a goatish wave.

Through the curtains—waves of water—
Comes the housekeeper's young daughter,

Where like coral-branches seem
The candles' light, the candles' gleam.

" Does Echo mourn her lost love there? "
Echo is a courtly air

Sighing the name of Cydalise
Beside clear pools of sleep; she sees

Her like a nymph in some deep grot
(Where the wave whispers not)

Like a rose-bush in that cave
Haunted by a goatish wave.

XV

Do, do,
Princess, do,
Like a tree that drips with gold you flow
With beauty ripening very slow.
Soon beneath that peaceful shade
The whole world dreaming will be laid.
Do, do.
Princess, do,
The years like soft winds come and go.

Do, do,
Princess, do,
How river-thick flow your fleeced locks
Like the nymphs' music o'er the rocks. . . .
From satyr-haunted caverns drip
These lovely airs on brow and lip.
Do, do,
Princess, do,
Like a tree that drips with gold you flow.

XVI

But far from snow-soft sleep, the country Fair
Spangled like planets the bucolic air
Under hot Capricorn, with gold goat-legs,
Rough satyr hands, that in the sunburnt hay
Pulled the long wind-blown hair of Susans, Megs,
And under great trees dark as water lay.

It semed a low-hung country of the blind,—
A sensual touch upon the heart and mind.
Like crazy creaking chalets hanging low
From the dark hairiness of bestial skies
The clouds seem, like a potting-shed where grow
The flower-like planets for the gay flower-show:
Gold-freckled calceolarias,
Marigolds, cinerarias,
African marigolds, coarse-frllled
And cherries, apricots, all chilled
With dew, for thus the bright stars seemed
To cottage windows where none dreamed.
But country gentlemen who from their birth,

Like kind red strawberries, root deep in earth
And sleep as in the grave, dream far beyond
The sensual aspects of the hairy sky
That something hides, they have forgotten why!
And so they wander, aiming with their gun
At mocking feathered creatures that have learnt
That movement is but groping into life,—
Under rough trees like shepherds' goatish tents.

And only Midsummer's wide country Fair
Seems to them heaven and hell, and earth and air.

The people ride in roundabouts; their hair
Is like the gardens of the Pleiades,
Or the first impulse from which music sprung,
And the dark sound in the smooth growth of trees;
They sparkle like the sea; their love is young
For ever, they are golden as the boy
Who gave an apple smoother than the breeze
To lady Venus, lovely as the seas;
Their lips are like the gold fires burning Troy.

Like harsh and crackling rags of laughter seems
The music, bright flung as an angel's hair—
Yet awful as the ultimate despair
Of angels and of devils. . . . Something dreams
Within the sound that shrieks both high and low
Like some ventriloquist's bright-painted show
On green grass, shrill as anger, dulled as hate:
It shrieks to the dulled soul, "Too late, too late!"
Sometimes it jangles thin as the sharp wires
Whereon the poor half-human puppets move;
Sometimes it flares in foliage like hell's fires,

Or whispers insincerities for love.
A little hurdy-gurdy waltz sounds hollow
And bright-husked as the hearts of passing people,
Whose talk is only of the growth of plums
And pears: "Life goes, Death never comes,"
They sigh, while the bright music like a wave
Sings of far lands and many a siren cave.

And there are terrible and quick drum-taps
That seem the anguished beat of our own heart
Making an endless battle without hope
Against materialism and the world.
And sometimes terrible lumbering Darkness comes
Breaking the trivial matchboard floors that hide
From us the Dead we dare not look upon:
O childish eyes, O cold and murdered face—
Dead innocence and youth that were our own!

But age has brought a little subtle change
Like the withdrawal caused by the slow dropping
Of cold sad water on some vast stone image:
A slow withdrawal, a sad, gradual change
O'er tragic masks through which strange gods have
    cried—
Till seen through death-cold rents in saturnine
    leaves
They seem, almost, to echo in their form
The saturnine cold laughter of the water.
And this, too, is the fate of country masks
Of Comedy, as fresh as smiling fruits
Of summer seen, vermilion, through deep leaves.

Now from the countrysides where people know
That Destiny is wingless and bemired,
With feathers dirty as a hen's, too tired
To fly—where old pig-snouted Darkness grovels
For life's mired rags among the broken hovels—
The country bumpkins come, with faces round
And pink as summer fruits, with hair as gold,
Sharp-pointed, as the summer sun (that old
Bucolic mime, whose laughing pantomime
Is rearing pink fruits from the sharp white rime).
They come from little rooms, each a poor booth
(Seen through the summer leaves, all smiling smooth).
There, for all beauty, is the badly painted
Ancestral portrait of their grey-beard God;
In that poor clownish booth it is so cold
That small airs prick like grass, a wooden sword.
They pass along the country roads as thick
With walls and gardens as a childish heaven,
Where all the flowers seem a pink fleshly heart
And mirage-dews sigh, " We will never part."
And there are young Princesses at each inn,
And poor young people poverty makes wise,
With eyes like maps of the wide summer heaven;
And on the country roads there is a shrine,
As blue and sparkling as the sea-god's wine,
For country gods and goddesses of gardens,
Where every fruit and flower to old songs hardens:
Pomona, tinsel-pink as that bright pear,
The moon—she seems a poor bucolic clown
With dry and gilded foliage for her hair,—
Where branches cast a shallow melancholy,
An owl-soft shadow falling over folly.
The pink schoolgirlish fruits hang in bright sheaves

Between the rounded and the negroid leaves. . . .
And we remember nursery afternoons
When the small music-box of the sweet snow
Gave half-forgotten tunes, and our nurse told
Us tales that fell with the same tinkling notes. . . .
" Once on a time," she said, " and long ago."
Her voice was sweet as the bright-sparkling rime,
The fruits are cold as that sweet music's time—
Yet all those fruits like the bright snow will fade.

The country bumpkins travel to the Fair,
For Night and Day, and Hell and Heaven, seem
Only a clown's booth seen in some bad dream,
Wherefrom we watch the movements of our life
Growing and ripening like summer fruits
And dwindling into dust, a mirage lie:
Hell is no vastness, it has naught to keep
But little rotting souls and a small sleep.
It has the same bright-coloured clarity we knew
In nursery afternoons so long ago,
Bright as our childish dreams; but we are old,
This is a different world; the snow lies cold
Upon our heart, though midsummer is here. . . .

XVII

But in the Court, the little people know
That Sleep is bright as fruit, and soft as snow.

The sunlight seems like warm brocade
In the courtyard, through the great arcade;

And golden as a Sultan's turban
The ripened medlars hang; the urban

Maids of the ladies at the palace
Talked like birds, with a gentle malice,

And on the wall, light-motes take shapes
Of vines, with showers of emerald grapes.

" Queen Venus is a toothless crone,
Blackened with age; all night alone

She lies, and no bird ever cries
For the wild starlight of her eyes."

" Once Helen was Prince Paris' doxy;
She meets her lovers now by proxy,

And wrinkled as the gold sea-sand
Are the breasts that once seemed heaven's land."

" Look at that little shadow . . . oh, the joy,
As black as any jewelled negro boy.

O little shade—see, I will call him Zambo.
Look where he silent sits, and plays dumbcrambo,

There at the door, with ghosts . . . and his mentero,
Half in brocaded sunlight, points to Zero!

Black fingers stretched to pluck the fruits of gold
Through the great leaves. . . . I feel a sudden cold

Sweet air from the arcade. . . . Again it goes.
The scented darkness seems as rich as snows,

Like cornucopias with ostrich plumes
And great gold fruits, the clouds seem from these
glooms."

Down in the great arcade of the courtyard
The fairies' coachmen, tawny as a pard,

Are talking of those feathered July eves
When all these dames desert their country leaves

(Though still as lovely as those moonlight maids
Juno and Dian, haunting their deep glades)—

And in their coach, with maids and footmen, drive
Up to the great town houses where they live;

No longer they seem fairies, but we see
Them named as the old Duchess of Bohea,

And Madam Cards, the Marchioness of Gout;
Though they are old, they still enjoy a rout,

And through the dark leaves of the shadow-grove,
As wickedly as ever, eyes still rove

That dealt death from behind a fluttered fan
In Pompeii, Athens, before Time began.

In courtyards stained with the black night like wine,
Strange figures with hair lifted like a vine

Listen. . . . Who is it hearkens at their doors,
In the vast rooms and endless corridors?

It is goat-footed, mincing Death, who presses
His muzzle at the keyhole, hears their dresses

Rustling like rose-leaves. . . . They hit him with their
fan,
Through scented moonlight move to their sedan.

When the hot gilded day will reach
A restful close,
A Japanese dwarf forest on the beach,
With dark trees of the shadow, the street grows.
How sand-like quivers the gold light
Under the large black leaves of shadow; mirage-bright
It lies, that dusty gold,
Untouched of any air;
Like Dead-Sea fruit carved in cornelian, bold,
The faces of a man and Pleasure's mournful daughter
Show lovely in the light, a moment flare,
Then shadows fall again—dark agates through clear
water.

Then these Chinoiseries, old ghosts of red and white
Smooth lacquer in their palanquins take flight

For tea, and the last esoteric rage
Whose plumes may soften age, that harpy's cage.

Their smile is like Death's trap . . . a little gilded dust
Of valueless beauty from the sun, soon must

Brush, for a fading while, each feathered cheek
That paradisal airs will never sleek,—

And round them, as they move, the unfading sea,
Eternity
With its cool feathered airs of beauty, sighs of no
horizons they can see.

What would these ghosts do, if the truths they know,
That were served up like snow-cold jewelled fruits,
And the enfeathered airs of lutes,
Could be their guests in cold reality?
They would be shivering,
Wide-eyed as a negro king
Seeing the evanescent mirage snow,—
They would be silenced by the cold
That is of the spirit, endlessly,
Unfabled, and untold.

The swan's breath winter these have known is finer
Fading than the early snows of China,

The poems of Queen Marguerite of Navarre,
(Narcissus-petalled, perfumed like a star)

Or the Pleiades' citron-scented poems, fading like the
snows,
Perfuming their long fingers till their eyelids close.

The winters these have known have been too kind,
With skies that seemed the bitter gilded rind

Of unattainable fruits; small women go
As white as ermines, and small winds are slow

As tunes upon a lute; the point-lace on the trees,
And the pearl-berries of the snow upon dark bushes
freeze,

And the snow falls, as sharp and bright, unripe and
sour,
As the budding grapes' bright perfume, or the sweet
grape-flower.

The daughters of the Silence now are dead,
And these Chinoiserie ghosts,
These mummies in dim hosts,
Tread the long mournful avenues instead;
Alarm the soul by their cold interest—
For what can be the purpose of their quest?

When spring begins, in China and Thibet
Through bell'd lime-avenues a springe is set
To catch the softly-smiling wind,
The cherubim to catch and blind
As cruel men blind a singing-bird;
They trap them with the sound of lutes
And the softest smiles of fruits,
That these old ghosts may prove the feathered
creatures real to hold,
And make them sing upon a perch of gold
In cages with a foolish bell-hung gable,
Amid the powders on their dressing-table;
Till, trapped by our mortality, they die, and their small
bones,

Sounding as sweetly as the west wind's tones,
Are sold because they sound like a small music-box;
Their slayers sell for silver the bright plumes in flocks,
To make the pillows for a sleepy head
That never dreams of heaven, but the lonely Dead.

And still they dwindle the bright world down to the gilded glooms
Of dust, these mummies, hieing, harrying fast
The Soul, their quarry, through the deserted tombs—
Or lying, lotus-eaters in a dreamful ease,
Perfuming their cold lips with silence and the past
Beneath the Asian darkness of smooth trees. . . .
Thus spoke the men; then sleep came colder than the rose
Blooming in desolation. . . . No one knows
The end there is to dust—it is the soul that shall survive them at the last.

XVIII

BENEATH a wan and sylvan tree
Whose water-flowing beauty our tired eyes
Can feel from very far, two travellers lie;
And one is swarthy as the summer wind,—
A man who travelled from a far country;
The other Soldan in his pomp and panoply
Seems like le Roi Soleil in all his pride,
When his gold periwig is floating wide.
They talked together, those dark kings beneath the bough,
And their songs mingled with soft winds that flow.

THE SOLDAN (*sings*)
" When green as a river was the barley,
Green as a river the rye,
I waded deep and began to parley
With a youth whom I heard sigh.
'I seek,' said he, 'a lovely lady,
A nymph as bright as a queen,
Like a tree that drips with pearls her shady
Locks of hair were seen;
And all the rivers became her flocks
Though their wool you cannot shear,
Because of the love of her flowing locks.
The kingly sun like a swain
Came strong, unheeding of her scorn,
Wading in deeps where she has lain,
Sleeping upon her river lawn
And chasing her starry satyr train.
She fled, and changed into a tree,—
That lovely fair-haired lady. . . .
And now I seek through the sere summer
Where no trees are shady!'

" They say that Daphne never was more fair
With all the shaken pearls of her long hair—
The lovely tree that was Apollo's love,
To whom he brought his richest spoils—than she!
And oh, that other Soldan, the hot sun
Burns not with love as I, with my dark pomp,
My helmet thick-plumed as a water-god's,
Whose cornucopia filled with dripping jewels
Is not so rich as treasuries I bear—
Dark spices, nard and spikenard, ambergris . . .
No maid will change into a tree before my kiss!"

" But I will be content with some far-lesser maid,
Who feeds her flocks beneath a fair-haired tree
And listens to the wind's song; she shall be
My soldanesse, and rule my far country.

(*He sings*)
Rose and Alice,
Oh, the pretty lassies,
With their mouths like a calice
And their hair a golden palace—
Through my heart like a lovely wind they blow.

Though I am black and not comely,
Though I am black as the darkest trees,
I have swarms of gold that will fly like honey-bees,
By the rivers of the sun I will feed my words
Until they skip like those fleecèd lambs
The waterfalls, and the rivers (horned rams),
Then for all my darkness I shall be
The peacefulness of a lovely tree—
A tree wherein the golden birds
Are singing in the darkest branches, oh! "

Thus sang those plumed kings, and the winds that flow
Whispered of lands no waking heart may know.

XIX

Now from the silk pavilions of the seas
The nymphs sing, gold and cold as orange-trees.

"Through gilded trellises
Of the heat, Dolores,
Inez, Manuccia,
Isabel, Lucia,
Mock Time that flies.
'Lovely bird, will you stay and sing,
Flirting your sheenèd wing,—
Peck with your beak, and cling
To our balconies?'
They flirt their fans, flaunting—
'O silence enchanting
As music!' then slanting
Their eyes,
Like gilded or emerald grapes,
They take mantillas, capes,
Hiding their simian shapes.
Sighs
Each lady, 'Our spadille
Is done.' . . . 'Dance the quadrille
From Hell's towers to Seville;
Surprise
Their siesta,' Dolores
Said. Through gilded trellises
Of the heat, spangles
Pelt down through the tangles
Of bell-flowers; each dangles
Her castanets, shutters
Fall while the heat mutters,
With sounds like a mandoline
Or tinkled tambourine. . . .
Ladies, Time dies!"

And petals of the foam, like perfumed orange-blossom,
Pelt the nymphs singing in their bowers—cold as their
bosom.

XX

In the hot noon—like glowing muscadine
The light seems, and the shade like golden wine—

Beneath the deep shade of the trees' arcade,
All foppish in his dressing-gown's brocade

And turban, comes the great Magnifico,
And hearkens not where the becafico

Time taps at the lovely sylvan trees.
Now underneath the shadows fallen from these

The queen sits with her court, and through the glade
The light from their silks casts another silver shade.

Home goes the great Magnifico, his dressing-gown
Is changed for water-rustling silks that drown

The shades, and walking proudly as the breeze
Now he advances through the sylph-slim trees.

" Madam, the Soldan and the King of Ethiop's land
Approach as suitors for your daughter's hand."

The day grew water-pale and cool as eves. . . .
A lady sang through water-rippling leaves:

" The mauve summer rain
Is falling again—
It soaks through the eaves
And the ladies' sleeves—
It soaks through the leaves

That like silver fish fall
In the fountains, recall
Afternoons when I
Was a child small and shy
In the palace. . . . Fish lie

On the grass with lives darkling.
Our laughter falls sparkling
As the mauve raindrops bright
When they fall through the light
With the briefest delight.
The pavilions float
On the lake like a boat. . . .
Mauve rains from trees fall
Like wysteria flowers . . . all
My life is like this
And drifts into nothingness!

The strange ladies sigh
' The autumn is nigh ' . . .
The King bows and mutters. . . .
His eyelids seem shutters
Of a palace pavilion
Deserted a million

Echoing years ago.
Oh, but the rain falls slow."

. . . . .

But no one heard the great Magnifico
Or this pale song, for underneath the low
Deep bough the queen slept, while the flowers that
fall
Seemed Ariadne's starry coronal.

XXI

In the great room above the orangery
The old queen's dwarfs are drinking their bohea

While the thin flames seem gold and whispering leaves
Of trees in the Hesperides, whose faint sound grieves.

So small, they could be hid in a pomander,
Miss Ellen and Sir Pompey Alexander

Seem . . . the tea is gold as evening,
The perfumes in the orangery sing,

And, flashing like exotic-plumaged birds,
The lovely shadows whisper unknown words.

Upon the wall, the portrait of Queen Anne
Frowned at them, and waved a languid fan,—

Queen Anne, whose white wig glittering in the net
Of gold light seems a florid bergerette,

Sheep-floury underneath the powder . . .
Her lips' small strawberry said " Louder "

To the shadows' fluttering bird . . .
But the lovely one scarce heard. . . .

The zephyrs' lips like ruffled roses sleek
Caressingly, each faintly upturned cheek;

And now the shutters like blue water
Fall . . . where is the King's daughter?

The candle-flames seem orange-flowers
Whose pale light falls in perfumed showers;

But Queen Anne, sleeping on the wall,
Long dead, would answer not at all.

XXII

The little golden lights like Chinese ladies peep
Through the old queen's curtains, then like sleep

Their gentle footsteps fade again and fail,
And once again the world is ghostly pale.

In the queen's powder-closet, Mrs. Troy
Teases the flames to wake them and annoy . . .

So pale are those thin ghostly flames that yet
They seem like the old notes of a spinet

That sometimes sounds a courante or gavotte
By Mozart or Scarlatti—sometimes not—

While the pale silken ribbons of the rain,
Knotted, are fluttering down the window-pane.

But suddenly the flames turn green and red
As unripe fruit; their shrilling fills her head

With noises like a painted puppet-show;
And in that music, shrieking high and low,

Dead is the pointed flames' small minuet—
And from the shrilling fire leaps Laidronette.

The ghostly apparition that appeared
Wagged from her chin a cockatrice's beard;

She crouches like a flame, the adder-sting
Of her sharp tongue is ready; hear her sing:

" The candle flames bob
Like strawberries low,
Bobcherry, bobcherry,
See them go
In the hands of the queen's maids
Under the trees
Of the shadow, flickering in the breeze.
Crept a starved and a humble air
From the hovels, grunting with low pig-snout,—
Starved thin, creeping
Everywhere, weeping
It blew the queen's strawberry candle-flames out.

The maids in long chequered gowns
Hunting for these
Find but the shadows'
Flickering trees.

The humble ghosts like poppet maids
Walk tiptoe in the shadow glades.

Their mouths seem small red strawberries;
Their naïve, naiad-titterings freeze

The airs in the long corridors
Where they must hark at hopeless doors.

And Mrs. Troy rose up like a thin shriek
Or pointed flame. . . . " Oh, my poor head is weak!

Oh dear,
Oh dear,
Whatever shall I do?
In the flames' shrill rout
Laidronette slipped through.
I forget the Latin
For my prayer!
My quilted satin
Is beyond repair!
I must tell the queen
But I dare not be seen!
Oh dear, oh dear,
I tremble with fear,
Like a nectarine bough
When the sun shines through.

How harmless has been my poor life—
Yet when a young girl, I had strife!
Out, alas! how I remember
That dawn, when to light the ember,

I must steal and I must creep
In the kitchen half asleep.
Noises from the sharp green wood
Burnt and bit my satyr blood,
And my cockscomb hair raised ire
In parrot-whistlers in the fire!

Now the ember as it dozes
Seems lattices of bunchèd roses,
Fuchsias and fat strawberries,
Dahlias, cherries, and one sees
Through those lattices' gold wire
The parrot-whistlers in the fire,
Pecking cherries every one.
'Polly, put the kettle on,'
Scream they; 'scratch poor pretty Polly'
(Kettles hissing at their folly!).
From the wood they spring and scream,
Scald the milk, upset the cream, . . .
Oh the feathers jewel-bright!
Alas! my life was never light."

The shrill flames nodded, beckoned, then lay dead;
Her wig awry, cross Poll Troy nods her head.

The long dark corridors seem shadow-groves
Wherein a little courtier air still roves. . . .

Pale rose-leaves, wet and scented, seems the rain,
Whose bright drops cease, as soft as sleep again.

Her gown seems like a pale and tuneful rose,

. . . .

Hours passed; the soft melodious moonlight
grows. . . .
A murmurous sound of far-off Circean seas
And old enchantments and the growth of trees.

. . . . .

Across the silver grass the powdered ghosts
Are wandering in dim and scattered hosts

Among the woods and fields, and they forget
Everything but that their love's hand yet
Is touching theirs; the ribbons of the moon are blue
And pink; those ghosts pick bunches from the dew

Of ghostly flowers, all poignant with spring rain,
Smelling of youth that will not come again.

XXIII

The public Scribe, noctambulo,
Where moonlight, cold as blades of grass
Echoes upon deserted walls
Turned his dusty folio. . . .
Dry grass that cackles thin in Hell
The spires of fire . . . his nightcap fell. . . .

Doctor Gradus
Mounts Parnassus
On that dusty ass the Law;
His hair is grey
As asses' ears,
The cold wind's bray
He never hears. . . .
O'er donkey's hide grass the attorney
Still continues on his journey

With the dusty Law's proceedings,
Through the old forrestial readings
For the Town of Troy
Prince Paris lost when yet a boy.

Il Dottore in the long grass
Culls the simples,—cold henbane,
Nettles that make fevers pass,
Wood-spurge that will cure a blain.

He walks where weeds have covered all. . . .
The moon's vast echoes die
Across the plain where weeds grown tall
Pearled treasuries of Asia seem,
Sunk in an endless dream.

And the mandarins in Asia,
In the silken palace of the moon,
Are all who are left to drink this physic
That will restore them from a swoon.

XXIV

NIGHT passed, and in that world of leaves
The Dawn came, rustling like corn-sheaves;

And a small wind came like little Boy-blue
Over the cornfield and rustling through
The large leaves. . . . Oh, how very deep
The old queen is sighing in her sleep:

" Alas, blue wind,
Bluebeard unkind,
Why have you blown so far from me
Through the jewelled blue leaves that sound like the
sea,

The lady Margotte,
The goosegirl Gargotte
Agog with curiosity?

They played Troy Town on the palace wall . . .
Like small grape hyacinths were their curls
And thin as the spring wind were those girls—
But now they never come if I call."

The kingly cock with his red-gold beard,
And his red-gold crown had crowed unheard

While his queens ruffled down
Their feathered gown
Beside the waterfall's crystal town;

The cock, the dawn-fruits, the gold corn,
Sing this aubade, cold, forlorn:

" Jane, Jane,
Forget the pain
In your heart. Go work again.

Light is given that you may
Work till owl-soft dusk of day.

The morning light whines on the floor, . . .
No one e'er will cross the door,

No one ever cares to know,
How ragged flowers like you do grow.

Like beaux and belles about the Court
King James the Second held, athwart

The field the sheep run,—foolish graces,
Periwigs, long Stuart faces,

While ragged-robin, cockscomb flowers
Cluck beneath the crystal showers.

A far-off huntsman sounds his horn
That sounds like rain, harsh and forlorn;

Pink as his coat, poor robin seems. . . .
Jane, no longer lie in dreams.

The crude pink stalactites of rain
Are sounding from the boughs again,

Each sighs the name of Harriet, Mary,
Susan, Anne, grown cold and wary—

Never your name. Bright and gay,
They used to whisper 'Come away,'

But now they have forgotten why.
Come, no longer sleeping lie.

Jane, Jane,
Forget the pain
In your heart. Go work again!"

No answer came. No footsteps now will climb
Down from Jane's attic. She forgets the time,
Her wages, plainness, and how none could love
A maid with cockscomb hair, in Sleep's dark grove.

XXV

And now the brutish forests close around
The beauty sleeping in enchanted ground.

All night, the harsh bucolic winds that grunt
Through those green curtains, help me in my hunt.

Oh the swinish hairy beasts
Of the rough wind
(Wild boars tearing through the forests)!
Nothing they will find

But stars like empty wooden nuts,
In leaves green and shrill.
Home they go to their rough stye
The clouds . . . and home go I.

Above the wooden shutters
Of my room at morn,
Like bunches of the country flowers
Seem the fresh dawn hours.

And the young dawn creeps
Tiptoe through my room, . . .
Never speaks of one who sleeps
In the forest's gloom.

XXVI

THE gardener played his old bagpipe
To make the melons and the peaches ripe. . . .
The threads are mixed in a tartan sound . . .
" Keep, my lad, to the good safe ground.
For Jonah long since was a felon,
With guineas gold as a grape or melon.
He always said his prayers in Latin
To peaches like red quilted satin;
And he had four and twenty daughters,
As lovely as the thick-fleeced waters
Or the Hesperides' thick-leaved trees—
And they were lovely as the evening breeze.
One Sabbath roamed that godless man
Beneath the great trees sylvan wan,
And met an ancient satyr crone,
Cold as the droning wind the drone
Hears when the thickest gold will thrive,
Summer-long, in the combs of the honey-hive.
She said, ' You must sail, as I understand,
Across the sea to a Better Land.'
The sea was sharper than green grass,
The sailors would not let him pass,
And the sea was wroth and rose at him
Like the turreted walls of Jerusalem,
Or like the towers and gables seen
In the midst of a deep-boughed garden green.
If my old bagpipe I blew
It would not blow those great towers down.
The sailors took and bound him, threw
Him in among those towers to drown.
And oh, far best," the gardener said,

" Like fruits to lie in your kind bed,
To sleep as snug as in the grave
In your kind bed, and shun the wave,
Nor ever sigh for a strange land
And songs no heart can understand."

THREE VARIATIONS ON A THEME

I

ROMANCE

FOR REE GORER

SHE grew within his heart as the flushed rose
In the green heat of the long summer grows
Deep in the sorrowful heaven of her leaves.
And this song only is the sound that grieves
When the gold-fingered wind from the green veins
Of the rich rose deflowers her amber blood,
The sharp green rains.
Such is the song, grown from a sleepy head,
Of lovers in a country paradise,—
You shall not find it where a song-bird flies,
Nor from the sound that in a bird-throat grieves,
Its chart lies not in maps on strawberry leaves.

Green were the pomp and pleasure of the shade
Wherein they dwelt; like country temples green
The huge leaves bear a dark-mosaic'd sheen
Like gold on forest temples richly laid.

And when the day first gleaned the sun's corn sheaves
The nymphs among those temples of the leaves
Hunted the boar; Zenobia and Aspasia
Were black beneath those great corn-sheaves like
Asia—

For the rich heat had made them black as cloud
Or smooth-leaved trees; they lay by waters loud,
And gold-stringed citherns of loud waters made
A madrigal, a country serenade.

In feathered head-dresses with bows and arrows
Beside the caves as green as gherkins, marrows,
Or gourds they walked; the Asian pomp and train
Of waves beside the glittering wide sea-main

They seemed, or like a fleet from India, fraught*
With all the riches of the rising sun
And precious sand from southern climates brought—
Rich as the tears from incense trees that run.

And there the satyr wind's long hands forlorn
Plucked the gold spangles of the dew from corn
And from the Asian darkness of the trees
To make more glittering the gowns of these,

Where swan-skin leaves of cherries seem a cloud
And coral tears of the rich light fall loud
In that smooth darkness; the gourds dark as caves
Hold thick gold honey for their fountains waves,

Figs dark and wrinkled as Silenus hold
Rubies and garnets, and the melons cold
Waves like a fountain; falling on the grass
The apples boom like sharp green summer rain.

*Dryden's "Annus Mirabilis."

But Time drifts by as the long-plumaged winds
And the dark swans whose plumes seem weeping leaves
In the shade's deepest splendour,—these drift by.
And sometimes he would turn to her and sigh:

"The bright swans leave the wave . . . so leave not
me.
With Aethiopǣa, smooth Aëropē
Amid the pomp and splendour of the shade
Their rich and leafy plumes a lulling music made.

Dark are their plumes, and dark the airs that grew
Amid those weeping leaves.
Plantations of the East drop precious dew
That ripened by the light, rich leaves perspire,
Such are the drops that from the bright swans'
feathers flew.

Come then, my pomp and pleasure of the shade,
Most lovely cloud that the hot sun made black
As dark-leaved swans.
Come then, O precious cloud,
Lean to my heart. No shade of some rich tree
Shall pour such splendour as your heart to me."

So these two lovers dreamed the time away
Beside smooth waters like the honey waves
In the ripe melons that are dark as caves;
Eternity seemed but a summer day.

And they forgot, seeing the Asian train
Of waves upon the glittering wide sea main
And rich gold waves from fountain caverns run,
That all the splendour of the eastern sun

And many a rose-shaped heart must lie beneath
The maps on strawberry leaves dark green as
snows,
With amber dust that was a nymph or rose—

And worlds more vast lie ruined by sad Time
That is the conqueror of our green clime.

For even the beasts eschew the shrunken heart
That dieth of itself, small deaths devour—
Or that worm mightier than death's,—the small
corroding hour.

How ancient is the Worm, companionless
As the black dust of Venus? Dulled to this
And loathèd as the Worm, she is alone
Though all the morbid suns lay in her kiss.

How old, the small undying snake that wreathes
Round lips and eyes, now that the kiss has gone?
In that last night, when we, too, are alone
We have, for love that seemed eternity
The old unchanging memory of the bone—
That porphyry whence grew the summer rose.

Most ancient is the Worm,—more old than night
Or the first music heard among the trees
And the unknown horizons' harmonies
Where the huge suns come freshened. Shrunk and
cold
Is he, like Venus blackened, noseless, old.

Yet all immensities lie in his strong
Embrace, horizons that no sight hath known,
The veins whose sea had heard the siren song
And worlds that grew from an immortal kiss.

And still their love amid this green world grieves:
" The gold light drips like myrrh upon the leaves
And fills with gold those chambers of the South
That were your eyes, that honeycomb your mouth.

And now the undying Worm makes no great stir,
His tight embrace chills not our luxuries
Though the last light perfumes our bones like myrrh
And Time's beat dies.
Come, with your kiss renew
The day till all the old worlds die like dew.

When the green century of summer rains
Lay on the leaves, then like the rose I wept.
For I had dwelt in sorrow as the rose
In the deep heaven of her leaves lies close.
Then you, my gardener, with green fingers stroked my
leaves
Till all the gold drops turned to honey. Grieves
This empire of green shade when honeyed rains
And amber blood flush all the sharp green veins
Of the rich rose?
So doth my rose-shaped heart
Feel the first flush of summer; love's first smart
Seemed no more sorrowful than the deep tears
The rose wept in that green and honeyed clime.

The green rains drip like the slow beat of Time
That grows within the amber blood, green veins
Of the rich rose, and in the rose-shaped heart,—
Changing the amber flesh to a clay wall.
Then comes the endless cold
At last, that is the Zero, mighty, old,
Huge as the heart, but than the worm more small—
Our final structure, the heart's ragged dress
That rose from Nothing, fell to Nothingness.

For the vast universal Night shall cover
The earth from Pole to Pole, and like a lover
Invade your heart that changed into my stone,
And I your Sisyphus. We two shall lie
Like those within the grave's eternity
And dream our arms hold the horizons deep
Where the strong suns come freshened from deep
seas,
The continents beyond discoveries,
Eternal youth, and the god's wisdom, sleep.

How should I dream that I must wake alone
With a void coffin of sad flesh and bone—
You, with the small undying serpent's kiss,
You, the dull rumour of the dust's renown—
The polar night, a boulder rolling down
My heart, your Sisyphus, to that abyss
Where is nor light, nor dark, nor soul, nor heart to
eat—
Only the dust of all the dead, the sound of passing
feet."

So winter fell, the heart shaped like the rose
Beneath the mountain of oblivion lies
With all death's nations and the centuries.
And this song ending fades like the shrill snows,

Dim as the languid moon's vast fading light
That scatters sparkles faint and dim and chill
Upon the wide leaves round my window sill
Like Aethiopæa ever jewelled bright . . .

So fading from the branches the snow sang
With a strange perfume, a melodious twang
As if a rose should change into a ghost—
A ghost turn to a perfume on the leaves.

II

METAMORPHOSIS

The coral-cold snow seemed the Parthenon,—
Huge peristyle of temples that are gone,
And dark as Asia, now, is Beauty's daughter
The rose, once clear as music o'er deep water.

Now the full moon her fire and light doth spill
On turkey-plumaged leaves and window-sill,

On leaves that seem the necks and plumes of urban
Turkeys, each a Sultan in a turban,

And strawberries among the beavers' wool,
(So grass seemed where that ruined temple's cool

Shade fell). When first the dew with golden foot
Makes tremble every leaf and strawberry root

The rainbow gives those berries light above,
The dark rose gives them all her secret love,

Until those coral tears of the rich light
Hold roses, rubies, rainbows for the sight.

My ancient shadow nods a turbaned head;
One candle through thick leaves throws a gold thread;

The dark green country temple of the snows
Hides porphyry bones of nymphs whence grew the rose,

And dark green dog-haired leaves of strawberries,
All marked with maps of unknown lands and seas,

And that small negro page, the cross dark quail,
Chasing the ghosts of dairymaids that fail

In butter-yellow dew by Georgian stables,
(The snow, dark green as strawberry leaves, has
gables).

But Time, a heavy ghost, groans through thick leaves,
Time is a weary bell which ever grieves:

It is not Death which is the skeleton—
But Time; Death merely strikes the hour of one,

Night's creeping end ere light begins again.
O Death has never worm for heart and brain

Like that which Time conceives to fill his grave,
Devouring the last faith, the word love gave,

Changing the light in eyes to heavy tears,
Changing the beat in heart to empty years

Wherein we listen for that little sound
Of footsteps that come never to our ground.

How terrible these winter nights must be
To the deserted Dead . . . if we could see

The eternal anguish of the skeleton,
So fleshless even the dog leaves it alone,

Atridæ-like devouring its own blood
With hopeless love beneath the earth's blind hood,
For warmth, the rags of flesh about the bone
Devoured by black disastrous dreams, alone

The worm is their companion, vast years
Pile mountain-high above, and the last tears

Freeze to gigantic polar nights of ice
Around the heart through crumbling centuries.

O Dead, your heart is gone, it cannot weep!
From decency the skeleton must sleep;

O heart, shrink out of sight, you have no flesh
For love or dog or worm to court afresh,

Only your youthful smile is mirrored lone
In that eternity, the skeleton.

For never come they now, nor comes the hour
When your lips spoke, and winter broke in flower,

The Parthenon was built by your dead kiss.
What should they seek, now you are changed to this

Vast craggy bulk, strong as the prophet's rock?
No grief tore waters from that stone to mock
Death's immobility, and changed to stone
Those eyelids see one sight and one alone.

What do they see? Some lost and childish kiss
In summers ere they knew that love was this,

The terrible Gehenna of the bone
Deserted by the flesh, tears changed to stone?

Or do they blame us that we walk this earth,
Who are more dead than they, nor seek rebirth

Nor change? The snowflake's six-rayed star can see
Rock-crystal's cold six-rayed eternity,—

Thus light grief melts in craggy waterfalls;
But mine melts never, though the last spring calls:

The polar night's huge boulder hath rolled this
My heart, my Sisyphus, in the abyss.

Do the Dead know the nights wherein we grope
From our more terrible abyss of hope
To soft despair? The nights when creeping Fear
Crumples our hearts, knowing when age appear,

Our sun, our love, will leave us more alone
Than the black mouldering rags about the bone?

Age shrinks our hearts to ape-like dust . . . that ape
Looks through the eyes where all death's chasms gape

Between ourself and what we used to be.
My soul, my Lazarus, know you not me?

Am I so changed by Time's appalling night?
'Tis but my bone that cannot stand upright,

That leans as if it thirsted . . . for what spring,
The ape's bent skeleton foreshadowing,

With head bent from the light, its only kiss?
Do the Dead know that metamorphosis,

When the appalling lion-claws of age
With talons tear the cheek and heart, yet rage

For life devours the bone, a tigerish fire?
But quenched in the vast empire of the mire

These craters cry not to the eternal bone:
The Dead may hide the changing skeleton.

So quench the light, my Lazarus, nor see
The thing we are, the thing that we might be:

In mouldering cerements of that thick grave,
Our flesh, we lose the one light that could save.

But yet it shall avail, that grass shall sing
From loveless bones in some foreshadowed spring,

And summer break from a long-shadowed kiss
Though our dry bones are sunless grown as this,

And eyeless statues, broken and alone
In shadeless avenues, the music gone,
We stand . . . the leaves we knew are black as jet,
Though the light scatters feathers on them yet,

Remembering sylvan nymphs . . . Death is our clime,
And, among heavy leaves, our bell to chime—

Death is our sun, illumining our old
Dim-jewelled bones—Death is our winter cold;

Yet sighs of voyages and landing stages
From unknown seas, and sylvan equipages,

And of a clime where Death's light on the eyes
Could make each shapeless lump of clay grow wise,

The topaz, sapphires, diamonds of the bone,
That mineral in our earth's dark mine, alone
Leap to the eastern light . . . Death-blinded eyes
See beyond wild bird-winged discoveries.

Death is the Sun's heat making all men black:
O Death, the splendours die in the leaves' track:

All men are Ethiopian shades of thee:
The wild and glittering fleece Parthenope

Loosened, more rich than feathers of bright birds,
Though rich and thick as Ethiopian herds

Died like the wave, or early light that grew
In eastern quarries ripening precious dew.*

Though lovely are the tombs of the dead nymphs
On the heroic shore, the glittering plinths
Of jacynth, hyacinthine waves profound
Sigh of the beauty out of sight and sound,

And many a golden foot that pressed the sand,
The panoply of suns on distant strand;

Panōpe walking like the pomp of waves
With plumaged helmet near the fountain caves

* Dryden's "Annus Mirabilis."

Is only now an arena for the worm;
Her golden flesh lies in the dust's frail storm,

And beauty water-bright for long is laid
Deep in the empire of eternal shade;

Only the sighing waves know now the plinth
Of those deep tombs that were of hyacinth.

Still echoes of that helmeted bright hair
Are like the pomp of tropic suns, the blare

That from the inaccessible horizon runs,
The eternal music of heroic suns
When their strong youth comes freshened from deep
seas,
And the first music heard among the trees.

By elephant trunks of the water, showers
Now change to cornucopias of flowers;

Panōpe with her dark majestic train
Of nymphs walked like the pomp of waves, the main

Sees Asia, Parthenope, Eunomia,
Euphrosyne, Urania, Ausonia,

In feathered head-dresses as bright as sleep,
As onward with the pomp of waves they sweep,

In pelongs, chelloes, and great palampores,
Gaze d'Ispahan and bulchauls, salampores,

In plumaged turbans, sweeping gros des Indes,
That the long golden fingers of the winds

Pull by the waters paler than a pearl.
The airs like rain-wet shrinking petals curl

And waves are freckled with gold ripples, these
Seem golden spangles on the strawberries;
And black Bacchantes with their panached feathers
Wear mittens with gold fringe bright as the weathers,

Where elephant trunks of the water rear
As the great pomp and train of nymphs draws near,

An ambassade of Amazons; rich trees
And Abyssinian glooms have fostered these.

But now Melpomene, Zenobia,
The Amazons black as Ethiopia

In Pan's huge forests seem like statues tall,
Where the thick jewels from the rich figs fall

In this vast empire of eternal shade
Where leaves seem Memphis, Thebes, from music
made.

In wooded gardens by each gardener's frame
Dark wrinkled satyrs with long straw beards came,

Dark honey from rough cups of straw to sip,
And every straw cup has an amber lip.

The gardener, wrinkled, dark, beside a cave
Sways branches gold-mosaic'd as the wave

And finds these are with satyrs' straw beards twined
By that gold-fingered arborist, the wind.

And there beside the greenest, shaggiest caves,
As green as melons hiding honey waves,

The rose that shone like the first light of tears
Was once a buskined bright nymph in lost years,

And from the amber dust that was a rose
In the green heat Parthenope still grows.

In this green world the melons' dogskin flowers,
Leaves green as country temples, snare the hours,

And dew seems butter-yellow, the bright mesh
Of dear and dead Panōpe's golden flesh

Where grapes and apples boom like emerald rain
In green baize forests, and the sylvan train

Of country nymphs wear yellow petticoats
Looped over leathern gaiters; long hair floats,
Cream-coloured and as thick as ponies' manes,
Through swan-soft great mauve leaves where Jove's
    gold rains

Still fly; rich strawberries are honeyed cold
By all Pan's honey and Palmyra's gold

And in the laughing green the rich fruits ran
With gilded honeyed blood of Phœbus, Pan.

But now the branches droop their melancholy
And owl-soft dusk upon this summer folly;

And under trees that were as fresh and green
As laughing nymphs' guitar and mandoline

(When country nymphs wore yellow petticoats
Looped over leathern gaiters, long hair floats

From straw hats trimmed with pheasants' feathers
twined
By the long golden fingers of the wind);

The broken country statue Corydon
Gilded by Phœbus, with his straw flute gone

Stands in the cocks of snow, once cocks of hay
Gilded and rustling o'er that green land lay;

And shadows brush the statue, not the snowy
Winged bees Sylvia and Thisbe, Chloe,

That sang sweet country songs in owl-dusked leaves:
" Poor Rose is dying " and " Sweet Sultan grieves."

But Time drifts owl-dusk o'er the brightest eyes
And dulls the sleepy gods and the sad wise,

And shall despoil our woods and monuments
And make them like the small bees' cerements . . .

And heavy is dark Time, that ever moans
Among thick leaves his mournful overtones.

Now the snow lies upon my rose-shaped heart,
And on the years, and many a glittering chart

The dog-furred strawberry leaves bear—maps from
dream
To dream—and berries with Orion's gleam.

This dark green country temple of the snows
Hides still the amber dust of nymph and rose,

The melons' dogskin flowers where the mellow,
Whining early dew is butter-yellow,

And the nymphs' smooth-eared hound, far from the
light,
When early dew whines hound-like as in fright.

I looked out from my window where the urban
Leaves seemed turkeys, (Sultans in a turban),
Across the lake where, cupolas and gables,
The ripples seemed deserted Georgian stables;

And my old shadow nods a turbaned head,
The full moon sees one candle's thick gold thread

Pierce through the thick leaves near the window sill,
Where she, her lovely fire and light doth spill.

The rose that shone like the first light of tears
Is faded, and its leaves, bright as the years

When we knew life and love and youth, are wet
With tears beneath the shady winter. Yet

Although the small immortal serpent cries
" I, only, know if Plato still be wise,

Great golden Hector had the pomp and pride
Of waves, but like the strength of these, he died;

And the first soundless wrinkles fall like snow
On many a golden cheek, and none may know,

Seeing your ancient wrinkled shadow-shape,
If this be long-dead Venus or an ape."

To patience with the apeish dust I came
Seeing this mimicry of death a game;
Since all things have beginnings; the bright plume
Was once thin grass in shady winter's gloom

And the furred fire is barking for the shape
Of hoarse-voiced animals; cold air agape

Whines to be shut in water's shape and plumes;
All this is hidden in the winter's glooms.

I too from ruined walls hung upside down
And, bat-like, only saw Death's ruined town

And mumbling crumbling dust . . . I saw the people
Mouthing blindly for the earth's blind nipple.

Their thick sleep dreams not of the infinite
Wild strength the grass must have to find the light

With all the bulk of earth across its eyes
And strength, and the huge weight of centuries.

Hate-hidden by a monk's cowl of ape's pelf,
Bear-clumsy and appalling, mine own self
Devouring, blinded by the earth's thick hood
I crouched, Atridæ-like devoured my blood

And knew the anguish of the skeleton
Deserted by the flesh, with Death alone.

Then my immortal Sun rose, Heavenly Love,
To rouse my carrion to life, and move

The polar night, the boulder that rolled this,
My heart, my Sisyphus, in the abyss.

Come then, my Sun, to melt the eternal ice
Of Death, and crumble the thick centuries,
Nor shrink, my soul, as dull wax owlish eyes
In the sun's light, before my sad eternities.

III

ELEGY ON DEAD FASHION

To Thomas Balston

Queen Venus' old historians seem like bees
That suck their honey from the thick lime-trees;
Behind their honeyed lattices all day,
As murmurous as thick-leaved lime-trees, they

Dream cells of Time away in murmuring o'er
The talk of little people gone before,
Within their palaces until gold eves
Bring them to windows in the tree-tops' leaves.

Manteaux espagnoles by the water's sheen,
Where trees resemble a great pelerine,
Are spread about the groups upon the lawns
Smooth as an almond's husk, or coat of fawns.

And cavaliers and ladies on the grass
Watch Chloe and young Damon as they pass,—
The shepherdess that runs from her swain's kiss,
Through leafy nets in a gown à l'Amadis

That rustles like the trembling evening,
Which falling on the lawns and brakes will bring
Roucoulement of doves, and veilèd belles
Preening their cloaks of cashmere tourterelles.

Oh, voices speaking by the waterfall!
Heroic statues cast a shadow tall,
And rustic faces where long water runs
Are now transformed to gold five-petalled suns.

But the historians murmur still like bees:
" How old is Venus? older than the trees,
Does she remember still the ancient bliss,
Grown dead and rotten, of Adonis' kiss?"

Through mulberry trees a candle's thick gold thread,—
So seems the summer sun to the sad Dead;
That cackling candle's loud cacophonies
Will wake not Plato, Aristophanes,

For all their wisdom. There in the deep groves
They must forget Olympus and their loves,
Lying beneath the coldest flower we see
On the young green-blooming strawberry.

The nymphs are dead like the great summer roses,
Only an Abyssinian wind dozes;
Cloyed with late honey are his dark wings' sheens,
Yet, once on these lone crags, nymphs bright as queens

Walked with elegant footsteps through light leaves,
Where only elegiac air now grieves,—
For the light leaves are sere and whisper dead
Echoes of elegances lost and fled.

Queen Thetis wore pelisses of tissue
Of marine blue or violet, or deep blue,
Beside the softest flower-bells of the seas.
In winter, under thick swan-bosomed trees

The colours most in favour were marine,
Blue Louise, gris bois, grenate, myrtle green;
Beside the ermine bells of the lorn foam—
Those shivering flower-bells—nymphs light-footed
roam

No more, nor walk within vast, bear-furred woods
Where cross owls mocked them from their leafy hoods,
And once, the ermine leaves of the cold snow
Seemed fashion leaves of eighty years ago.—

When first as thin as young Prince Jamie's plaid
The tartan leaves upon the branches laid
Showed feathered flowers as brown as any gannet,
And thin as January or as Janet,—

Chione, Cleopatra, Boreas' daughters
Walked beside the stream's drake-plumaged waters
In crinolines of plaided sarsenet,
Scotch caps, where those drake-curling waters wet

Their elegant insteps.—Household nymphs must
wear
For humble tasks the ponceau gros d'hiver,—
(Tisiphone the Fury, like a dire
Wind raising up Balmoral towers of fire).

Another wind's small drum through thin leaves
taps,
And Venus' children wearing their Scotch caps
Or a small toque Hongroise that is round-brimmed,
And with a wing from Venus' pigeons trimmed,

Run now with hoops and dolls they call " cher cœur,"
Chase Cupid in his jacket artilleur,
Play on the cliffs where like the goats' thick locks
The coarse grass grows, and clamber on the rocks.

Above the forest, whence he shot the does,
Was Jupiter's vast shooting-box of snows—
His blunderbuss's ancient repercussions
Fired but pears and apples, furred as Russians.

He threw his gun down and began to curse,
When up ran Venus' children with their nurse:
" See, Grandpapa, rocks like Balmoral's towers
Held still these brown and gannet-plumaged flowers."

Then underneath the hairy and the bestial
Skies of winter ripening, a celestial
Bucolic comedy of subtle meaning
Grew with rough summer suns, until with preening

Of soft bird-breasted leaves, again we knew
The secret of how hell and heaven grew.
Where walked great Jupiter, and like a peasant
Shot the partridge, grouse, and hare, and pheasant,

In the gods' country park there was a farm
Where all the gentle beasts came to no harm,
Left to run wild. And there in that great wood
Was Juno's dairy, cold as any bud,

With milk and cream, as sweet and thick as yellow
Apricots and melons, in the mellow
Noon when dairy maids must bear it through
Lanes full of trilling flowers and budding dew.

And then beside the swanskin pool where pansies
And strawberries and other pretty fancies
With the wild cherries sing their madrigals,
The goddesses walked by the waterfalls;

But now beside the water's thin flower-bells
No bustles seem rose castles and tourelles
Beside the little lake that seems of thin
And plumeless and too delicate swanskin;

Nor sparks and rays from calèche wheels that roll
Mirror the haycocks with gilt rays like Sol
Where trees seemed icebergs,—rose and green
reflections
Of the passing nymphs and their confections.—

In summer, when nymph Echo was serene
On these lone crags walked many a beauteous
queen
As lovely as the light and spangled breeze
Beside the caves and myrtle groves and trees.

One wood-nymph wore a deep black velvet bonnet
With blackest ivy leaves for wreaths upon it,—
Shading her face as lovely as the fountains
While she descended from deep-wooded mountains,

And with the wood-gods hiding, Charlottine,
Boreas' daughter, wore a crinoline.
So fair with water-flowing hair was she,
That crinoline would shine from crag and tree.

When the gold spangles on the water seen
Were like the twanging of a mandoline,
And all the ripples were like ripest fruits
That grow from the deep water's twisted roots,

The water-nymph, dark Mademoiselle Persane,
On blond sands wore an Algerine turbane;
Of blue velours d'Afrique was the pelisse
Of Grisi the ondine, and like the fleece

Of water gods, or gold trees on the strand,
Her gold hair fell like fountains on the sand,—
The thick gold sand beside the siren waves,—
Like honey-cells those sands and fountain caves.

Dream of the picnics where trees, sylvan, wan,
Shaded our feasts of nightingale and swan,
With wines as plumed as birds of paradise,
Or Persian winds, to drown the time that flies!

Then, on the shaven ice-green grass one sees
Roses and cherries and ripe strawberries
Bobbing at our lips like scarlet fire
Between the meshes of the light's gold wire,

And the bacchantes with their dew-wet hair,
Like velvety dark leaves of vineyards, wear
Great bunchèd tufts of African red coral
Whose glints with sheen of dew and leaves now quarrel.

Here in a sheep-thick shade of tree and root
Nymphs nurse each fawn whose pretty golden foot
Skipped there. They, milk of flaxen lilies, sip
From a sweet cup that has a coral lip,

In that green darkness. Melons dark as caves
Held thick gold honey for their fountain waves,
And there were gourds as wrinkled dark as Pan,
Or old Silenus,—figs whence jewels ran.

There in the forest, through the green baize leaves,
Walked Artemis, and like the bound-up sheaves
Of gilt and rustling-tressèd corn, her arrows
Through greenhouses of vegetable marrows

She aimed; like the vast serres-chaudes of the lake,
Those greenhouses, her arrows then did break!
Her dress was trimmed with straw, her hair streamed
bright
And glittering as topaz, chrysolite.

Among their castles of gold straw entwined
With blackest ivy buds and leaves, and lined
With lambs' wool, and among the cocks of hay,
The satyrs danced the sheep-trot all the day

And sometimes stole a gherkin and a marrow,
Some strawberries, and a cucumber narrow,
Where the straw-coloured harsh leaves hid the
root,
And only showed the scarlet glistening fruit.

In wooded gardens where the green baize leaves
Hid fruit that rustled like Ceres' gilt sheaves
They danced the galloppade and the mazurka,
Cracoviak, cachucha, and the turka,

With Fauna and the country deities,
Pan's love Eupheme, and the Hyades,—
Phaola and Ambrosia and Eudora,
Panōpe and Eupompe with great Flora,

Euryale, the Amazonian queen
Whose gown is looped above the yellow sheen
Of her bright yellow petticoat,—the breeze
Strewed wild flowers on her straw hat through the
    trees;

And country nymphs with round straw hats deep-
    brimmed,
And at one side with pheasants' feathers trimmed,—
With gowns of green mohair and high kid boots
Wherewith they trample radish, strawberry, roots.

But far are we from forests of our rest
Where the wolf Nature from maternal breast
Fed us with strong brown milk . . . those epochs gone,
Our eyeless statues weep from blinded stone.

And far are we from the innocence of man,
When Time's vast sculptures from rough dust began,
And natural law and moral were but one,—
Derived from the rich wisdom of the sun.

In those deep ages the most primitive
And roughest and uncouthest shapes did live
Knowing the memory of before their birth,
And their soul's life before this uncouth earth.

We could remember in that ancient time
Of our primeval innocence, a clime
Divined deep in the soul, in which the light
Of vaster suns gave wisdom to our sight;

Now, days like wild beasts desecrate each part
Of that forgotten tomb that was our heart;
There are more awful ruins hanging there
Than those which hang and nod at empty air.

Yet still our soul keeps memories of that time
In sylvan wildernesses,—our soul's prime
Of wisdom, forests that were Gods' abode,
And Saturn marching in the Dorian mode.

But all the nymphs are dead. The sound of fountains
Weeps swan-soft elegies to the deep mountains,—
Repeats their laughter, mournful now and slow,
To the dead nymph Echo. Long ago

Among the pallid roses' spangled sheens
On these lone crags nymphs that were bright as queens
Walked with elegant footsteps through light leaves
Where now a dark-winged southern wind soft grieves,

So cloyed with honey he must close his wing.
No ondine Grisi now may rise to sing,
For the light leaves are sere and whisper dead
Echoes of elegances lost and fled.

The nymphs are dead. And yet when spring begins
The nation of the Dead must feel old sins
Wake unremembering bones, eternal, old
As Death. Oh, think how these must feel the cold

In the deep groves! But here these dead still walk
As though they lived, and sigh awhile, and talk.
O perfumed nosegay brought for noseless Death!
This brightest myrrh can not perfume that breath.

The nymphs are dead,—Syrinx and Dryope
And that smooth nymph that changed into a tree.
But though the shade, that Ethiopia, sees
Their beauty make more bright its treasuries,

Their amber blood in porphyry veins still grows
Deep in the dark secret of the rose,
Though dust are their bright temples in the heat,
The nymph Parthenope with golden feet.

My glittering fire has turned into a ghost,
My rose is now cold amber and is lost;
Yet from that fire you still could light the sun,
And from that amber, bee-winged motes could
come;

Though grown from rocks and trees, dark as Saint
Anne,
The little nun-like leaves weep our small span,
And eyeless statues in the garden weep
For Niobe who by the founts doth sleep,

In gardens of a fairy aristocracy
That lead downhill to mountain peaks of sea,
Where people build like beavers on the sand
Among life's common movements, understand

That Troy and Babylon were built with bricks;
They engineer great wells into the Styx
And build hotels upon the peaks of seas
Where the small trivial Dead can sit and freeze.

Still ancient fanfares sound from mountain gorges
Where once Prometheus lit enormous forges:
"Debout les morts!" No key when the heart closes:
The nymphs are dead like the great summer roses.

But Janet, the old wood-god Janus' daughter,
All January-thin and blond as water,
Runs through the gardens, sees Europa ride
Down to the great Swiss mountains of the tide,

Though in the deep woods, budding violets
And strawberries as round as triolets
Beneath their swanskin leaves feel all alone. . . .
The golden feet that crushed them now are gone.

Beside the Alps of sea, each crinoline
Of muslin and of gauze and grenadine
Sweeps by the Mendelssohnian waterfall,
O'er beaver-smooth grass, by the castle wall,

Beside the thick mosaic of the leaves.
Left by the glamour of some huger eves
The thick gold spangles on those leaves are seen
Like the sharp twanging of a mandoline;

And there, with Fortune, I too sit apart
Feeling the jewel turn flower, the flower turn heart,
Knowing not goddess's from beggar's bones,
Nor all death's gulf between those semitones.

We who were proud and various as the wave,—
What strange companions the unreasoning grave
Will give us . . . wintry Prudence's empty skull
May lie near that of Venus the dead trull!

There are great diamonds hidden in the mud
Waiting Prometheus' fire and Time's vast flood,
Wild glistening flowers that spring from these could
know
The secret of how hell and heaven grow.

But at a wayside station near the rock
Where vast Prometheus lies, another bock
Is brought by Ganymede . . . why dream the
Flood
Would save those diamonds hidden in the mud?

The farmer on his donkey now rides down
The mountain side with angels' eggs the town
Will buy, beside the mountain peaks of sea
And gardens of the fairy aristocracy,

And ladies in their carriages drive down
The mountain to the gardens of the town,
And the hot wind, that little Savoyard,
Decked them with wild flowers à la montagnard.

The wood-nymphs Nettie, Alexandrine, tear
Balmoral gowns made for this mountain wear,—
White veils; each Fauchon-emigré bonnet
Bears coronets of berries wild upon it;

Huge as the great gold sun, each parasol
That hides it; fluid zephrys now extol
Antiope's short bell-shaped pelerine
Worn lest gauze ribbons of the rain be seen.

" Oh the blond hair of Fortune in the grove!
Lean from your carriage, hold her lest she rove!"
" Her face is winter, wrinkled, peaceless, mired,
Black as the cave where Cerberus was sired.—

O soul, my Lazarus! There was a clime
Deep in your tomb of flesh, defying time,
When a god's soul played there, began to dance
Deep in that tomb with divine, deathless Chance.

But that huge god grew wearied of our game
And all the lion-like waterfalls grew tame.
Venus, a statue mouldering on the wall,
Noseless and broken now, forgetting all

The fanfares, knows that Phœbus gilds her still
On pastoral afternoons; but she is chill.
Venus, you too have known the anguished cold,
The crumbling years, the fear of growing old!

Here in this theatre of redistributions,
This old arena built for retributions,
We rose imperial from primeval slime
Through architecture of our bones by Time;

Now night like lava flows without a chart
From unremembering craters of the heart,
Anguished with their dead fires.—Beneath the caves
And crags the Numidean sibyl raves;

We hear the sibyl crying Prophecy:
' There where the kiss seems immortality
I prophesy the Worm . . . there, in the kiss,
He'll find his most imperial luxuries.' "

. . . . .

Where mountains, millers' dusty bags, seem full
Of Priam's gold, and all the black sheep's wool
Of thunderstorms, and grass in forests floats
As green as Tyrolean peasants' petticoats,

Dead Venus drove in her barouche, her shawl
As mauve as mountain distance covering all,
As she swept o'er the plain with her postillions
That were black and haughty as Castillians.

There, high above the thickest forests were
The steepest high-walled castles of the air;
And paths led to those castles that were bordered
With great gardens, neat and walled and ordered

With rivers, feathered masks, and pots of peas
Mournful beneath the vast and castled trees,
Where gardeners clip the strange wind's glittering
    fleece.
Oh, how that wind can blow through a pelisse!

Miss Ellen and Miss Harriet, the ondines,
Bore baskets full of velvet nectarines
And walnuts, over wooden trellissed bridges
That cross the streams and the steep mountain ridges.

They wore straw-coloured crinolines of faille
Beneath their shady bonnets made of paille,—
Their melancholy laughter ever sounds
Through castled trees and over castle grounds.

But I am sad, and by the wrinkled lake,
Where the great mauve flowers will never wake,
But drip with sleep and dew, I read this thin,
Dry, withered book of delicate swanskin,

And find a tale of an Olympian glade
Where Psyche has become a kitchenmaid;
The world, that pitiful old catchpenny,
Whines at her booth for pence, and finds too many,

Showing the gods no larger than ourselves,
And twittering bird-like from the rocky shelves
Of this Olympus, and no prophecy
They roar, but whisper triviality.

The ancient castle wall of Chaos nods.
Through gaps of ruined air and withered pods
A showman came; he smiles like Time and mocks
Me, takes his marionettes from their small box,—

The gods, Time-crumbled into marionettes.
Death frays their ageless bodies, hunger frets
Them, till at last, like us, they dance
Upon the old dull string pulled now by Chance.

This is the game the apeish shuddering dust
Plays for the market and the house of lust;
There are a thousand deaths the spirit dies
Unknown to the sad Dead that we despise.

Still ladies in their carriages drive down
The mountain to the gardens of the town,
And the hot wind, that little Savoyard,
Decked them with wild flowers à la montagnard.

Rich as a tomb each dress! oh, pity these!
I think the rich died young, and no one sees
The young loved face show for a fading while
Through that death-mask, the sad and cynic smile.

. . . . .

These living skeletons blown by the wind
Were Cleopatra, Thais . . . age unkind
Has shrunken them so feeble and so small
That Death will never comfort them at all.

They are so poor they seem to have put by
The outworn fashion of the flesh! They lie
Naked and bare in their mortality
Waiting for Death to warm them, childishly.

Do these Dead, shivering in their raggedness
Of outworn flesh, know us more dead, and guess
How day rolls down, that vast eternal stone,
Shuts each in his accustomed grave, alone?

Round the eternal skeleton their dress
Is rags, our mountain-high forgetfulness
Through centuries is piled above the Dead,
Waiting in vain for some remembered tread

Upon this rock-bound march that all we made
To the eternal empire of the shade,—
To the small sound of Time's drum in the heart.
The sound they wait for dies, the steps depart.

Come not, O solemn and revengeful Dead,—
Most loving Dead, from your eternal bed
To meet this living ghost, lest you should keep
Some memory of what I was, and weep.

FIVE SONGS

To my Sister Georgia

1.—DAPHNE

Heat of the sun that maketh all men black,—
They are but Ethiopian shades of thee—
Pour down upon this wild and glittering fleece
That is more rich than feathers of bright birds,
The ripening gems, the drops of the still night.
I parch for that still shade, my heat of love
That parched those ripening gems hath withered me.

Come with the African pomp and train of waves,
Give me your darkness, my immortal shade,
Beside the waterwells my heart hath known.
The shepherds hairy-rough as satyrs come,
Bring up their fleeces that are waterfull
With freshness clear as precious gums of trees
Where weep the incense trees from some deep smart,
So the fresh water from your fleece flows in
To fill with richness all my desert heart.

2.—THE SYLPH'S SONG

" The cornucopia of Ceres
I seek not, fading not for these,

But fair Pomona, gardener's daughter,
Laughing like bird-feathered water.

Amid this hot green glowing gloom
A word falls with a rain-drop's boom;

And baskets of ripe fruit in air
The bird-songs seem, suspended where

Those goldfinches, the ripe warm lights,
Peck slyly at them, take quick flights.

I bring you branches green with dew
And fruits that you may crown anew

Your waspish-gilded hair until
That cornucopia doth spill

Dew, and your warm lips bear the stains,
And bird-blood leap within your veins.

Pomona, lovely gardener's daughter,
Fruits like ripples of the water

Soon will fade . . . then leave your fruits,
Smooth as your cheek or the birds' flutes,

And in this lovelier smoother shade
Listen to my serenade."

3.—THE PEACH TREE

Between the amber portals of the sea
The gilded fleece of heat hangs on my tree;
My skin is bright as this . . .
Come, wind, and smooth my skin, bright as your kiss!

Less bright, less bright than Fatima's gold skin,
My gilded fleece that sighs
' She is the glittering dew born of the heat,
She is that young gazelle, the leaping Sun of Paradise.'

Come, Nubian shade, smooth the gilt fleece's curl,
Until your long dark fluid hands unfold
My peach, that cloud of gold,
Its kernel, crackling amber water-cold.

Shine, Fatima, my Sun, show your gold face
Through panached ostrich plumes of leaves, then from
above
My ripening fruits will feel the bright dew fall apace,
Till at your feet I pour my golden love.

4.—THE STRAWBERRY

BENEATH my dog-furred leaves you see
The creeping strawberry
In a gold net
The footprints of the dew have made more wet.

Mahomet resting on a cloud of gold
Dreamed of the strawberry
Made of the purpling gauzy heat
And jasper dust trod by his golden feet,—

The jasper dust beside
The fountain tide,

The water jacynth-cold,
The water-ripples like mosaics gold
Have made my green leaves wide and water-cold.

From palaces among the widest leaves
My Sun, my Fatima,
Shows her gold face and sighs,
And darkness dies.

At noon my Fatima, my bright gazelle,
Walks by each gauzy bell
Of strawberries made of such purpling air
As the heat knows, and there

When Fatima, my dew with golden foot,
Comes like all the music of the air
Then shine my berries till those golden footsteps die—
Like all the glittering desert of the air when the hot
sun goes by.

5.—THE GREENGAGE TREE

From gold-mosaic'd wave
And from the fountain cave
Grew my dark-plumaged leaves all green and fountain-
cold,
My minarets of gold,

Mosaic'd like the tomb,
Far in the forest gloom,
Of water-lovely Fatima in forests far away.
The gardener doth sway

The branches and doth find
(As wrinkled dark and kind
As satyrs) these with satyrs' straw beards twined
By that gold-fingered arborist the wind.

Among thick leaves the shade
Seems like a cavalcade,
Or Artemis plume-helmeted from sylvan serenade,
Or Amazons' ambassade.

A Caliph plays a lute,
A gardener plays a flute,
Then from my feathered stem a most delightful gust,
    a glittering sea
Grows in my rich fruit.

And each bird-angel comes
To sip dark honey from my plums,
My rich green amber gums
That make puffed feather sleeves, long feathered skirts
    all gold,
And sticky from the dew my golden net doth hold.

FOUR ELEGIES

I.—The Heart and the Hambone

TO PAVEL TCHELITCHEW

A Girl speaks:

" Here in this great house in the barrack square,
The plump and heart-shaped flames all stare
Like silver empty hearts in wayside shrines.
No flame warms ever, shines,
Nor may I ever tire.

Outside, the dust of all the dead,
Thick on the ground is spread
Covering the tinsel flowers
And pretty dove-quick hours,

Among the round leaves, Cupid-small
Upon the trees so wise and tall.
O dust of all the dead, my heart has known
That terrible Gehenna of the bone
Deserted by the flesh,—with Death alone!

Could we foretell the worm within the heart,
That holds the households and the parks of heaven,
Could we foretell that land was only earth,
Would it be worth the pain of death and birth,
Would it be worth the soul from body riven?

For here, my sight, my sun, my sense,
In my gown white as innocence,
I walked with you. Ah, that my sun
Loved my heart less than carrion.

Alas! I dreamed that the bare heart could feed
One who with death's corruption loved to breed,—
This Dead, who fell, that he might satisfy
The hungry grave's blind need,—

That Venus stinking of the Worm!
Deep in the grave, no passions storm:
The worm's a pallid thing to kiss;
She is the hungering grave that is

Not filled, that is not satisfied!
Not all the sunken Dead that lies
Corrupt there, chills her luxuries.

And fleet, and volatile her kiss,
For all the grave's eternities!
And soon another Dead shall slake
Her passion, till that dust, too, break.

Like little pigeons small dove-breasted flowers,
Were cooing of far-off bird-footed showers,
My coral neck was pink as any rose
Or like the sweet pink honey-wax that grows,
Or the fresh coral beams of clear moonlight,
Where leaves like small doves flutter from our
 sight.

Beneath the twisted rose-boughs of the heat
Our shadows walked like little foreigners,
Like small unhappy children dressed in mourning,
They listened by the serres-chaudes waterfalls
But could not understand what we were saying,
Nor could we understand their whispered warning.—
There by the waterfalls we saw the Clown,
As tall as Heaven's golden town,
And in his hands, a Heart, and a Hambone
Pursued by loving vermin; but deserted, lone,
The Heart cried to my own:

The Heart speaks:

Young girl, you dance and laugh to see,
The thing that I have come to be.
Oh, once this heart was like your own.
Go, pray that yours may turn to stone.

This is the murdered heart of one
Who bore and loved an only son.
For him, I worked away mine eyes,
My starved breast could not still his cries.

My little lamb, of milk bereft . . .
My heart was all that I had left.
Ah, could I give thee this for food,
My lamb, thou knowest that I would.

Yet lovely was the summer light
Those days . . . I feel it through this night.
Once Judas had a childish kiss,
And still his mother knows but this.

He grew to manhood. Then one came,
False-hearted as Hell's blackest shame
To steal my child from me, and thrust
The soul I loved down to the dust.

Her hungry wicked lips were red
As that dark blood my son's hand shed;
Her eyes were black as Hell's own night;
Her ice-cold breast was winter-white.

I had put by a little gold
To bury me when I was cold.
That fangèd wanton kiss to buy,
My son's love willed that I should die.

The gold was hid beneath my bed,—
So little, and my weary head
Was all the guard it had. They lie
So quiet and still who soon must die.

He stole to kill me while I slept,
The little son who never wept,
But that I kissed his tears away
So fast, his weeping seemed but play.

So light his footfall. Yet I heard
Its echo in my heart and stirred
From out my weary sleep to see
My child's face bending over me.

The wicked knife flashed serpent-wise,
Yet I saw nothing but his eyes
And heard one little word he said,
Go echoing down among the Dead.

. . . . .

They say the Dead may never dream.
But yet I heard my pierced heart scream
His name within the dark. They lie
Who say the Dead can ever die.

For in the grave I may not sleep,
For dreaming that I hear him weep.
And in the dark, my dead hands grope
In search of him. O barren hope!

I cannot draw his head to rest,
Deep down upon my wounded breast;
He gave the breast that fed him well
To suckle the small worms of Hell.

The little wicked thoughts that fed
Upon the weary helpless Dead,
They whispered o'er my broken heart,—
They struck their fangs deep in the smart:

" The child she bore with bloody sweat
And agony has paid his debt.
Through that bleak face the stark winds play,
The crows have chased his soul away,—

His body is a blackened rag
Upon the tree,—a monstrous flag,"
Thus one worm to the other saith.
Those slow mean servitors of Death,

They chuckling, said: " Your soul grown blind
With anguish, is the shrieking wind
That blows the flame that never dies
About his empty lidless eyes."

I tore them from my heart, I said:
" The life-blood that my son's hand shed—
That from my broken heart outburst,
I'd give again to quench his thirst.

He did no sin. But cold blind earth
The body was that gave him birth.
All mine, all mine the sin. The love
I bore him was not deep enough."

. . . . .

The Girl speaks:
O crumbling heart, I too, I too have known
The terrible Gehenna of the bone
Deserted by the flesh . . . . I too have wept
Through centuries like the deserted bone
To all the dust of all the Dead to fill
That place. . . . It would not be the dust I loved.

For underneath the lime-tree's golden town
Of Heaven, where he stood, the tattered Clown
Holding the screaming Heart and the Hambone,
You saw the Clown's thick hambone, life-pink carrion,
That Venus perfuming the summer air.
Old pigs, starved dogs, and long worms of the grave
Were rooting at it, nosing at it there.
Then you, my sun, left me and ran to it
Through pigs, dogs, grave-worms' ramparted tall
waves.

. . . . .

I know that I must soon have the long pang
Of grave-worms in the heart. . . . You are so
 changed,
How shall I know you from the other long
Anguishing grave-worms? I can but foretell
The worm where once the kiss clung, and that last
 less chasm-deep farewell.

2.—The Little Ghost who Died for Love

FOR ALLANAH HARPER

Deborah Churchill, born in 1678, was hanged in 1708 for shielding her lover in a duel. His opponent was killed, her lover fled to Holland, and she was hanged in his stead, according to the law of the time. The chronicle said, "Though she died at peace with God, this malefactor could never understand the justice of her sentence, to the last moment of her life."

" Fear not, O maidens, shivering
As bunches of the dew-drenched leaves
In the calm moonlight . . . . it is the cold sends
 quivering
My voice, a little nightingale that grieves.

Now Time beats not, and dead Love is forgotten . . .
The spirit too is dead and dank and rotten,

And I forget the moment when I ran
Between my lover and the sworded man—
Blinded with terror lest I lose his heart.
The sworded man dropped, and I saw depart

Love and my lover and my life . . . he fled
And I was strung and hung upon the tree.
It is so cold now that my heart is dead
And drops through time . . . night is too dark to see

Him still. . . . But it is spring; upon the fruit-boughs
of your lips,
Young maids, the dew like India's splendour drips;
Pass by among the strawberry beds, and pluck the
berries
Cooled by the silver moon; pluck boughs of cherries

That seem the lovely lucent coral bough
(From streams of starry milk those branches grow)
That Cassopeia feeds with her faint light,
Like Ethiopia ever jewelled bright.

Those lovely cherries do enclose
Deep in their sweet hearts the silver snows,

And the small budding flowers upon the trees
Are filled with sweetness like the bags of bees.

Forget my fate . . . but I, a moonlight ghost,
Creep down the strawberry paths and seek the lost

World, the apothecary at the Fair.
I, Deborah, in my long cloak of brown
Like the small nightingale that dances down
The cherried boughs, creep to the doctor's bare
Booth . . . cold as ivy in the air,

And, where I stand, the brown and ragged light
Holds something still beyond, hid from my sight.

Once, plumaged like the sea, his swanskin head
Had wintry white quills . . . ' Hearken to the Dead . . .
I was a nightingale, but now I croak
Like some dark harpy hidden in night's cloak,
Upon the walls; among the Dead, am quick;
Oh, give me medicine, for the world is sick;
Not medicines, planet-spotted like fritillaries
For country sins and old stupidities,
Nor potions you may give a country maid
When she is lovesick . . . love in earth is laid,
Grown dead and rotten ' . . . so I sank me down,
Poor Deborah in my long cloak of brown.
Though cockcrow marches, crying of false dawns,
Shall bury my dark voice, yet still it mourns
Among the ruins,—for it is not I
But this old world, is sick and soon must die!"

3.—The Lament of Edward Blastock

FOR RICHARD ROWLEY

Note.—I took this story from the "Newgate Calendar." Edward Blastock suffered at Tyburn on the 26th of May, 1738. Being in the direct want, and seeing his sister and her children in an equal misery, he yielded to the solicitations of his sister's husband, and joined with him in becoming highwaymen. They went so far as to rob a gentleman of a few shillings. Then Edward Blastock, finding a warrant was out against him, took refuge in his sister's house.

She betrayed him to his death.

The pang of the long century of rains,
Melting the last flesh from the bone,
Cries to the heart: "At least the bone remains,—
If this alone."

My bone cries to my mother's womb:
Why were you not my tomb?
Why was I born from the same womb as she
Who sold my heart, my blood, who stole even my
grave from me?

I crept to steal in the rich man's street
That my sister's starving babes might eat—

(Death, you have known such rags as hold
The starved man's heart together,—Death, you have
known such cold!)

I crept to hide in my sister's room,
And dreamed it safe as my mother's womb:

But there was a price upon the head
Of one who stole that her babes might feed,

So my sister said, "I must go to buy
Us bread with this pence. . . ." And, for this, I die
—Beyond my Death . . . with no grave to lie

In, hide my heart deep down in that hole.
For my sister went to sell her soul

And my heart, and my life, and the love I gave. . . .
She went to rob me of my grave.

And I would, I would the heart I gave
Were dead and mouldering in that grave,

I would that my name were forgot,
And my death dead beneath Death's rot.

But I'd give the last rag of my flesh
About my heart to the endless cold
Could I know again the childish kiss
My Judas gave of old—
Oh, Christ that hung between two men like me,—
Could I but know she was not this,—not this!

4.—The Ghost whose Lips were Warm

"T. M., Esq., an old acquaintance of mine, hath assured me, that . . . after his first wife's death, as he lay in bed awake . . . his wife opened the Closet Door, and came into the Chamber by the Bed side, and looked upon him and stooped down and kissed him; her Lips were warm, he fancied they would have been cold. He was about to have Embraced her, but was afraid it might have done him hurt. When she went from him, he asked her when he should see her again? She turned about and smiled, but said nothing."—Miscellanies collected by John Aubrey, Esq., F.R.S., 1696.

FOR GEOFFREY GORER

"The ice, weeping, breaks.
But my heart is underground.
And the ice of its dead tears melts never. Wakes
No sigh, no sound,

From where the dead lie close, as those above—
The young—lie in their first deep night of love,

When the spring nights are fiery with wild dew, and
rest
Leaves on young leaves, and youthful breast on breast.

The dead lie soft in the first fire of spring
And through the eternal cold, they hear birds sing,

And smile as if the one long-treasured kiss
Had worn away their once-loved lips to this

Remembered smile—for there is always one
Kiss that we take to be our grave's long sun.

Once Time was but the beat of heart to heart;
And one kiss burnt the imperfect woof apart

Of this dead world, and summer broke from this:
We built new worlds with one immortal kiss.

Sun of my life, she went to warm the dead,
And I must now go sunless in their stead.

They clothed a dead man in my dress. By day
He walks the earth, by night he rots away;

So walks a dead man, waning, in my dress,
By black disastrous suns of death grown less,

Grown dim and shrunken, wax before a fire,
A shrunken apeish thing, blackened and dire.

This black disastrous sun yet hath no heat.
How shall I bear my heart without its beat,

My clay without its soul, my eternal bone
That cries to its deserting flesh, alone,

More cold than she is in her grave's long night,
That hath my heart for covering, warmth, and light.

. . . . .

But when she had been twelve months in her grave
She came where I lay in my bed: she gave

Her kiss. And oh, her lips were warm to me.
And so I feared it, dared not touch and see

If still her heart were warm . . . dust-dun, death-cold
Lips should be from death's night. I dared not hold

That heart that came warm from the grave . . . afraid
I tore down all the earth of death, and laid

Its endless cold upon her heart. For this
Dead man in my dress dared not kiss

Her who laid by death's cold, lest I
Should feel it when she came to lie

Beside my heart. My dead love gave
Lips warm with love though in her grave:

I stole her kiss, the only light
She had to warm her eternal night."

COLONEL FANTOCK

To Osbert and Sacheverell

Thus spoke the lady underneath the trees:
I was a member of a family
Whose legend was of hunting—(all the rare
And unattainable brightness of the air)—
A race whose fabled skill in falconry
Was used on the small song-birds and a winged
And blinded Destiny. . . . I think that only
Winged ones know the highest eyrie is so lonely.
There in a land, austere and elegant,
The castle seemed an arabesque in music;
We moved in an hallucination born
Of silence, which like music gave us lotus
To eat, perfuming lips and our long eyelids
As we trailed over the sad summer grass,
Or sat beneath a smooth and mournful tree.

And Time passed, suavely, imperceptibly.

But Dagobert and Peregrine and I
Were children then; we walked like shy gazelles
Among the music of the thin flower-bells.
And life still held some promise,—never ask
Of what,—but life seemed less a stranger, then,
Than ever after in this cold existence.
I always was a little outside life,—
And so the things we touch could comfort me;

I loved the shy dreams we could hear and see—
For I was like one dead, like a small ghost,
A little cold air wandering and lost.

All day within the straw-roofed arabesque
Of the towered castle and the sleepy gardens wandered
We; those delicate paladins the waves
Told us fantastic legends that we pondered.

And the soft leaves were breasted like a dove,
Crooning old mournful tales of untrue love.

When night came, sounding like the growth of trees,
My great-grandmother bent to say good night,
And the enchanted moonlight seemed transformed
Into the silvery tinkling of an old
And gentle music-box that played a tune
Of Circean enchantments and far seas;
Her voice was lulling like the splash of these.
When she had given me her good-night kiss,
There, in her lengthened shadow, I saw this
Old military ghost with mayfly whiskers,—
Poor harmless creature, blown by the cold wind,
Boasting of unseen unreal victories
To a harsh unbelieving world unkind,—
For all the battles that this warrior fought
Were with cold poverty and helpless age—
His spoils were shelters from the winter's rage.
And so for ever through his braggart voice,
Through all that martial trumpet's sound, his soul
Wept with a little sound so pitiful,
Knowing that he is outside life for ever
With no one that will warm or comfort him. . . .

He is not even dead, but Death's buffoon
On a bare stage, a shrunken pantaloon.
His military banner never fell,
Nor his account of victories, the stories
Of old apocryphal misfortunes, glories
Which comforted his heart in later life
When he was the Napoleon of the schoolroom
And all the victories he gained were over
Little boys who would not learn to spell.

All day within the sweet and ancient gardens
He had my childish self for audience—
Whose body flat and strange, whose pale straight hair
Made me appear as though I had been drowned—
(We all have the remote air of a legend)—
And Dagobert my brother whose large strength,
Great body and grave beauty still reflect
The Angevin dead kings from whom we spring;
And sweet as the young tender winds that stir
In thickets when the earliest flower-bells sing
Upon the boughs, was his just character;
And Peregrine the youngest with a naïve
Shy grace like a faun's, whose slant eyes seemed
The warm green light beneath eternal boughs.
His hair was like the fronds of feathers, life
In him was changing ever, springing fresh
As the dark songs of birds . . . the furry warmth
And purring sound of fires was in his voice
Which never failed to warm and comfort me.

And there were haunted summers in Troy Park
When all the stillness budded into leaves;
We listened, like Ophelia drowned in blond

And fluid hair, beneath stag-antlered trees;
Then, in the ancient park the country-pleasant
Shadows fell as brown as any pheasant,
And Colonel Fantock seemed like one of these.
Sometimes for comfort in the castle kitchen
He drowsed, where with a sweet and velvet lip
The snapdragons within the fire
Of their red summer never tire.
And Colonel Fantock liked our company;
For us he wandered over each old lie,
Changing the flowering hawthorn, full of bees,
Into the silver helm of Hercules,
For us defended Troy from the top stair
Outside the nursery, when the calm full moon
Was like the sound within the growth of trees.

But then came one cruel day in deepest June,
When pink flowers seemed a sweet Mozartian tune,
And Colonel Fantock pondered o'er a book.
A gay voice like a honeysuckle nook,—
So sweet,—said, " It is Colonel Fantock's age
Which makes him babble." . . . Blown by winter's
rage
The poor old man then knew his creeping fate,
The darkening shadow that would take his sight
And hearing; and he thought of his saved pence
Which scarce would rent a grave . . . that youthful
voice
Was a dark bell which ever clanged " Too late "—
A creeping shadow that would steal from him
Even the little boys who would not spell,—
His only prisoners. . . . On that June day
Cold Death had taken his first citadel.

FAÇADE

To Sacheverell

"*This modern world is but a thin match-board flooring spread over a shallow hell. For Dante's hell has faded, is dead. Hell is no vastness; here are no more devils who laugh or who weep—only the maimed dwarfs of this life, terrible straining mechanisms, crouching in trivial sands, and laughing at the giant's crumbling !*"—From an essay by the Author.

I.—Père Amelot

The stars like quaking-grass grow in each gap
Of air (ruined castle wall) . . .
Père Amelot in his white nightcap
Peered through . . . saw nothing at all.

Like statues green from the verdigris
Of the moon, two shadows join
His shade, that under that castle wall sees
The moon like a Roman coin.

Out of his nightcap he drew three pence . . .
Marie and Angélique pass
The knife through Père Amelot's back—in the dense
Bushes fly . . . he nods on the grass.

The man with the lanthorn, a moment after,
Picks up the moon that fell
Like an Augustan coin when laughter
Shook the hen-cackling grass of Hell;

And the Public Writer inscribing his runes
Beneath that castle wall, sees
Three Roman coins as blackened as prunes—
And Père Amelot slain for these!

The stars like quaking-grass grow in each gap
Of air—ruined castle wall . . .
Père Amelot nods in his white nightcap . . .
He knows there is nothing at all!

2.—CLOWNS' HOUSES

BENEATH the flat and paper sky
The sun, a demon's eye,
Glowed through the air, that mask of glass;
All wand'ring sounds that pass

Seemed out of tune, as if the light
Were fiddle-strings pulled tight.
The market-square with spire and bell
Clanged out the hour in Hell,

The busy chatter of the heat
Shrilled like a parokeet;
And shuddering at the noonday light
The dust lay dead and white

As powder on a mummy's face,
Or fawned with simian grace
Round booths with many a hard bright toy
And wooden brittle joy:

The cap and bells of Time the Clown
That, jangling, whistled down,
Young cherubs hidden in the guise
Of every bird that flies;

And star-bright masks for youth to wear,
Lest any dream that fare
—Bright pilgrim—past our ken, should see
Hints of Reality.

Upon the sharp-set grass, shrill-green,
Tall trees like rattles lean,
And jangle sharp and dizzily;
But when night falls they sigh

Till Pierrot moon steals slyly in,
His face more white than sin
Black-masked, and with cool touch lays bare
Each cherry, plum, and pear.

Then underneath the veilèd eyes
Of houses, darkness lies,—
Tall houses; like a hopeless prayer
They cleave the sly dumb air.

Blind are those houses, paper-thin;
Old shadows hid therein,
With sly and crazy movements creep
Like marionettes, and weep.

Tall windows show Infinity;
And, hard reality,
The candles weep and pry and dance
Like lives mocked at by Chance.

The rooms are vast as Sleep within:
When once I ventured in,
Chill Silence, like a surging sea
Slowly enveloped me.

3.—LULLABY FOR JUMBO

JUMBO asleep!
Grey leaves thick-furred
As his ears, keep
Conversations blurred.
Thicker than hide
Is the trumpeting water;
Don Pasquito's bride
And his youngest daughter
Watch the leaves
Elephantine grey:
What is it grieves
In the torrid day?
Is it the animal
World that snores
Harsh and inimical
In sleepy pores?—
And why should the spined flowers
Red as a soldier
Make Don Pasquito
Seem still mouldier?

4.—TRIO FOR TWO CATS AND A TROMBONE

LONG steel grass—
The white soldiers pass—

The light is braying like an ass.
See
The tall Spanish jade
With hair black as nightshade
Worn as a cockade!
Flee
Her eyes' gasconade
And her gown's parade
(As stiff as a brigade).
Tee-hee!
The hard and braying light
Is zebra'd black and white
It will take away the slight
And free
Tinge of the mouth-organ sound,
(Oyster-stall notes) oozing round
Her flounces as they sweep the ground.
The
Trumpet and the drum
And the martial cornet come
To make the people dumb—
But we
Won't wait for sly-foot night
(Moonlight, watered milk-white, bright)
To make clear the declaration
Of our Paphian vocation,
Beside the castanetted sea,
Where stalks Il Capitaneo
Swaggart braggadocio
Sword and moustachio—
He
Is green as a cassada
And his hair is an armada.

To the jade : " Come kiss me harder ! "
He called across the battlements as she
Heard our voices thin and shrill
As the steely grasses' thrill,
Or the sound of the onycha
When the phoca has the pica
In the palace of the Queen Chinee!

5.—MADAME MOUSE TROTS

" Dame Souris trotte gris dans le noir."—VERLAINE.

MADAME MOUSE trots,
Grey in the black night!
Madame Mouse trots:
Furred is the light.
The elephant-trunks
Trumpet from the sea . . .
Grey in the black night
The mouse trots free.
Hoarse as a dog's bark
The heavy leaves are furled . . .
The cat's in his cradle,
All's well with the world!

6.—FOUR IN THE MORNING

CRIED the navy-blue ghost
Of Mr. Belaker
The allegro negro cocktail-shaker,
" Why did the cock crow,
Why am I lost,
Down the endless road to Infinity toss'd?

The tropical leaves are whispering white
As water; I race the wind in my flight.
The white lace houses are carried away
By the tide; far out they float and sway.
White is the nursemaid on the parade.
Is she real, as she flirts with me unafraid?
Such honeyed imbecility lies
In the eternal July skies
As in her giggling curls. In swirls
The houses fade, and drop in pearls.
I raced through the leaves as white as water . . .
Ghostly, flowed over the nursemaid, caught her,
Left her . . . edging the far-off sand
Is the foam of the sirens' Metropole and Grand,
And along the parade I am blown and lost,
Down the endless road to Infinity toss'd.
The guinea-fowl plumaged houses sleep . . .
On one, I saw the lone grass weep,
Where only the whimpering greyhound wind
Chased me, raced me, for what it could find."
And there in the black and furry boughs
How slowly, coldly, old Time grows,
Where the pigeons smelling of gingerbread,
And the spectacled owls so deeply read,
And the sweet ring-doves of curded milk,
Watch the Infanta's gown of silk
In the ghost-room tall where the governante
Gesticulates lente, and walks andante.
" Madam, Princesses must be obedient;
For a medicine now becomes expedient,—
Of five ingredients,—a diapente,"
Said the governante, fading lente . . .
In at the window then looked he,

The navy-blue ghost of Mr. Belaker,
The allegro negro cocktail-shaker,—
And his flattened face like the moon saw she,—
Rhinoceros-black (a flowing sea!).

7.—" I DO LIKE TO BE BESIDE THE SEASIDE "

WHEN
Don
Pasquito arrived at the seaside
Where the donkey's hide tide brayed, he
Saw the banditto Jo in a black cape
Whose slack shape waved like the sea—
Thetis wrote a treatise noting wheat is silver like the sea; the lovely cheat is sweet as foam; Erotis notices that she
Will
Steal
The
Wheat-king's luggage, like Babel
Before the League of Nations grew—
So Jo put the luggage and the label
In the pocket of Flo the Kangaroo.
Through trees like rich hotels that bode
Of dreamless ease fled she,
Carrying the load and goading the road
Through the marine scene to the sea.
" Don Pasquito, the road is eloping
With your luggage, though heavy and large;
You must follow and leave your moping
Bride to my guidance and charge! "

When
Don
Pasquito returned from the road's end,
Where vanilla-coloured ladies ride
From Sevilla, his mantilla'd bride and young friend
Were forgetting their mentor and guide.
For the lady and her friend from Le Touquet
In the very shady trees upon the sand
Were plucking a white satin bouquet
Of foam, while the sand's brassy band
Blared in the wind. Don Pasquito
Hid where the leaves drip with sweet . . .
But a word stung him like a mosquito . . .
For what they hear, they repeat!

8.—SAID THE NOCTAMBULO

BENEATH the gilt capricorn
Said the Noctambulo
Turning his folio
To the papillio
By the night born:
" I nod my head
And the great Avatar
With his scented guitar
And his scimitar,
Pretends to be dead;
And my snore forlorn
Is a horn
That will blow
Down the gilt capricorn
And the walled Jericho."

9.—CAME THE GREAT POPINJAY

CAME the great Popinjay
Smelling his nosegay:
In cages like grots
The birds sang gavottes.
" Herodiade's flea
Was named sweet Amanda,
She danced like a lady
From here to Uganda.
Oh, what a dance was there!
Long-haired, the candle
Salome-like tossed her hair
To a dance-tune by Handel" . . .
Dance they still? Then came
Courtier Death,
Blew out the candle-flame
With civet breath.

10.—TWO VARIATIONS ON AN OLD NURSERY RHYME

THE KING OF CHINA'S DAUGHTER

I

THE King of China's daughter,
She never would love me
Though I hung my cap and bells upon
Her nutmeg tree.
For oranges and lemons,
The stars in bright blue air,
(I stole them long ago, my dear)
Were dangling there.

The moon did give me silver pence,
The sun did give me gold,
And both together softly blew
And made my porridge cold;
But the King of China's daughter
Pretended not to see
When I hung my cap and bells upon
Her nutmeg tree.

II

THE King of China's daughter
So beautiful to see
With her face like yellow water, left
Her nutmeg tree.
Her little rope for skipping
She kissed and gave it me—
Made of painted notes of singing-birds
Among the fields of tea.
I skipped across the nutmeg grove,—
I skipped across the sea;
But neither sun nor moon, my dear,
Has yet caught me.

11.—BLACK MRS. BEHEMOTH

IN a room of the palace
Black Mrs. Behemoth
Gave way to wroth
And the wildest malice.
Cried Mrs. Behemoth,
" Come, court lady,
Doomed like a moth,
Through palace rooms shady!"

The candle flame
Seemed a yellow pompion,
Sharp as a scorpion,
Nobody came . . .
Only a bugbear
Air unkind
That bud-furred papoose,
The young spring wind,
Blew out the candle.
Where is it gone?
To flat Coromandel
Rolling on!

12.—THE AVENUE

In the huge and glassy room
Pantaloon, with his tail-feather
Spangled like the weather,
Panached, too, with many a plume,
Watched the monkey Fanfreluche,
Shivering in his gilded ruche,
Fawn upon the piano keys,
Flatter till they answer back
Through the scale of centuries,
Difference between white and black.
Winds like hurricanes of light
Change the blackest vacuums,
To a light-barred avenue—
Semitones of might and right;
Then, from matter, life comes.

Down that lengthy avenue
Leading us we know not where,
Sudden views creep through the air;
Oh, the keys we stumble through:
Jungles splashed with violent light,
Promenades all hard and bright,
Long tails like the swish of seas,
Avenues of piano keys!
Meaning comes to bind the whole,
Fingers separate from thumbs,
Soon the shapeless tune comes:
Bestial efforts at man's soul,
What though notes are false and shrill—
Black streets tumbling down a hill?
Fundamentally
I am you, and you are me—
Octaves fall as emptily.

13.—MARINER MEN

"What are you staring at, mariner-man,
Wrinkled as sea-sand and old as the sea?"
"Those trains will run over their tails, if they can,
Snorting and sporting like porpoises. Flee
The burly, the whirligig wheels of the train,
As round as the world and as large again,
Running half the way over to Babylon, down
Through fields of clover to gay Troy town—
A-puffing their smoke as grey as the curl
On my forehead as wrinkled as sands of the sea!—
But what can that matter to you, my girl?
(And what can that matter to me?)"

14.—THE SATYR IN THE PERIWIG

THE Satyr Scarabombardon
Pulled periwig and breeches on:
" Grown old and stiff, this modern dress
Adds monstrously to my distress.
The gout within a hoofen heel
Is very hard to bear; I feel
When crushed into a buckled shoe
The twinge will be redoubled, too;
And when I walk in gardens green
And, weeping, think on what has been,
Then wipe one eye,—the other sees
The plums and cherries on the trees.
Small bird-quick women pass me by
With sleeves that flutter airily,
And baskets blazing like a fire
With laughing fruits of my desire:
Plums sunburnt as the King of Spain,
Gold-cheeked as any Nubian,
With strawberries all goldy-freckled,
Pears fat as thrushes and as speckled.
Pursue them? . . . Yes, and squeeze a tear:
' Please spare poor Satyr one, my dear! '
' Be off, sir! Go and steal your own! '
—Alas, poor Scarabombardon,
Trees rend his ruffles, stretch a twig,
Tear off a satyr's periwig! "

15.—THE OWL

THE currants, moonlit as Mother Bunch,
In their thick-bustled leaves were laughing like Punch;

And, ruched as their country waterfalls
The cherried maids walk beneath the dark walls.
Where the moonlight was falling thick as curd
Through the cherry-branches, half-unheard,
Said old Mrs. Bunch, the crop-eared owl,
To her gossip: " If once I began to howl,
I am sure that my sobs would drown the seas
With my ' ohs,' and my ' ahs,' and my ' oh dear mes ! '
Everything wrong from cradle to grave—
No money to spend, no money to save! "
And the currant-bush began to rustle
As poor Mrs. Bunch arranged her bustle.

16.—TWO WALTZES

I—WATER PARTY

Rose Castles
Those bustles
Beneath parasols seen!
Fat blondine pearls
Rondine curls
Seem. Bannerols sheen
The brave tartan
Waves' Spartan
Domes—(Crystal Palaces)
Where like fallacies
Die the calices
Of the water-flowers green.
Said the Dean
To the Queen,
On the tartan wave seen:
" Each chilly

White lily
Has her own crinoline,
And the seraphs recline
On divans divine
In a smooth seventh heaven of polished pitch-pine."
Castellated,
Related
To castles the waves lean
Balmoral-like;
They quarrel, strike
(As round as a rondine)
With sharp towers
The water-flowers
And, floating between,
Each châtelaine
In the battle slain—
Laid low by the Ondine.

2.—SYLPH'S SONG

" DAISY and Lily,
Lazy and silly,
Walk by the shore of the wan grassy sea,—
Talking once more 'neath a swan-bosomed tree.
Rose castles,
Tourelles,
Those bustles
Where swells
Each foam-bell of ermine,
They roam and determine
What fashions have been and what fashions will be,—
What tartan leaves born,
What crinolines worn.

By Queen Thetis,
Pelisses
Of tartlatine blue,
Like the thin plaided leaves that the castle crags grew,
Or velours d'Afrande:
On the water-gods' land
Her hair seemed gold trees on the honey-cell sand
When the thickest gold spangles, on deep water seen,
Were like twanging guitar and like cold mandoline,
And the nymphs of great caves,
With hair like gold waves,
Of Venus, wore tarlatine.
Louise and Charlottine
(Boreas' daughters)
And the nymphs of deep waters,
The nymph Taglioni, Grisi the ondine,
Wear plaided Victoria and thin Clementine
Like the crinolined waterfalls;
Wood-nymphs wear bonnets, shawls,
Elegant parasols
Floating are seen.
The Amazons wear balzarine of jonquille
Beside the blond lace of a deep-falling rill;
Through glades like a nun
They run from and shun
The enormous and gold-rayed rustling sun;
And the nymphs of the fountains
Descend from the mountains
Like elegant willows
On their deep barouche pillows,
In cashmere Alvandar, barège Isabelle,
Like bells of bright water from clearest woodwell.
Our élégantes favouring bonnets of blond,

The stars in their apiaries,
Sylphs in their aviaries,
Seeing them, spangle these, and the sylphs fond
From their aviaries fanned
With each long fluid hand
The manteaux espagnoles,
Mimic the waterfalls
Over the long and the light summer land.

. . . . .

So Daisy and Lily,
Lazy and silly,
Walk by the shore of the wan grassy sea,
Talking once more 'neath a swan-bosomed tree.
Rose castles,
Tourelles,
Those bustles!
Mourelles
Of the shade in their train follow.
Ladies, how vain,—hollow,—
Gone is the sweet swallow,—
Gone, Philomel!"

17.—HORNPIPE

Sailors come
To the drum
Out of Babylon;
Hobby-horses
Foam, the dumb
Sky rhinoceros-glum

Watch the courses of the breakers' rocking-horses and with Glaucis,
Lady Venus on the settee of the horsehair sea!

Where Lord Tennyson in laurels wrote a gloria free,
In a borealic iceberg came Victoria; she
Knew Prince Albert's tall memorial took the colours of
    the floreal
And the borealic iceberg; floating on they see
New-arisen Madam Venus for whose sake from far
Came the fat and zebra'd emperor from Zanzibar
Where like golden bouquets lay far Asia, Africa, Cathay,
All laid before that shady lady by the fibroid Shah.
Captain Fracasse stout as any water-butt came, stood
With Sir Bacchus both a-drinking the black tarr'd
    grapes' blood
Plucked among the tartan leafage
By the furry wind whose grief age
Could not wither—like a squirrel with a gold star-nut.
Queen Victoria sitting shocked upon the rocking horse
Of a wave said to the Laureate, " This minx of course
Is as sharp as any lynx and blacker-deeper than the
    drinks and quite as
Hot as any Hottentot, without remorse!
            For the minx,"
                        Said she,
            " And the drinks,
                        You can see
Are hot as any Hottentot and not the goods for me! "

18.—WHEN SIR BEELZEBUB

When
Sir
Beelzebub called for his syllabub in the hotel in Hell
            Where Proserpine first fell,
Blue as the gendarmerie were the waves of the sea,
            (Rocking and shocking the bar-maid).

Nobody comes to give him his rum but the
Rim of the sky hippopotamus-glum
Enhances the chances to bless with a benison
Alfred Lord Tennyson crossing the bar laid
With cold vegetation from pale deputations
Of temperance workers (all signed In Memoriam)
Hoping with glory to trip up the Laureate's feet,
(Moving in classical metres) . . .
Like Balacalava, the lava came down from the
Roof, and the sea's blue wooden gendarmerie
Took them in charge while Beelzebub roared for his
rum.
. . . None of them come!

TWENTY-SIX BUCOLIC COMEDIES

To Arnold Bennett

"*Countrysides where the people know that Destiny is befouled and has feathers like a hen . . . landscapes where the leaves have an animal fleshiness, and old pig-snouted Darkness grunts and roots in the hovels. There, the country gentlemen are rooted in the mould; and they know that beyond the sensual aspect of the sky (that harsh and goatish tent) something hides—but they have forgotten what it is. So they wander, aiming with their guns at mocking feathered creatures that have learnt the wonder and secret of movement, beneath clouds that are so low-hung that they seem nothing but wooden potting-sheds for the no-longer disastrous stars . . . (they will win the prize at the local flower-show). The water of the shallow lake gurgles like a stoat, murderously; the little unfledged feathers of the foam have forgotten how to fly, and the country gentleman wanders, hunting for something—hunting!*"—From an essay by the Author.

I.—EARLY SPRING

The wooden châlets of the cloud
Hang down their dull blunt ropes to shroud

Red crystal bells upon each bough
(Fruit-buds that whimper). No winds slough

Our faces, furred with cold like red
Furred buds of satyr springs, long dead!

The cold wind creaking in my blood
Seems part of it, as grain of wood;

Among the coarse goat-locks of snow
Mamzelle still drags me to and fro;

Her feet make marks like centaur hoofs
In hairy snow; her cold reproofs

Die, and her strange eyes look oblique
As the slant crystal buds that creak.

If she could think me distant, she
In the snow's goat-locks certainly

Would try to milk those teats, the buds,
Of their warm sticky milk—the cuds

Of strange long-past fruit-hairy springs—
Beginnings of first earthy things!

2.—SPRING

When spring begins, the maids in flocks
Walk in soft fields, and their sheepskin locks

Fall shadowless, soft as music, round
Their jonquil eyelids, and reach the ground.

Where the small fruit-buds begin to harden
Into sweet tunes in the palace garden,

They peck at the fruit-buds' hairy herds
With their lips like the gentle bills of birds.

. . . . .

But King Midas heard the swan-bosomed sky
Say " All is surface and so must die."

And he said: " It is spring; I will have a feast
To woo eternity; for my least

Palace is like a berg of ice;
And the spring winds, for birds of paradise,

With the leaping goat-footed waterfalls cold,
Shall be served for me on a dish of gold

By a maiden fair as an almond-tree,
With hair like the waterfalls' goat-locks; she

Has lips like that jangling harsh pink rain,
The flower-bells that spirt on the trees again."

In Midas' garden the simple flowers
Laugh, and the tulips are bright as the showers,

For spring is here; the auriculas,
And the Emily-coloured primulas

Bob in their pinafores on the grass
As they watch the gardener's daughter pass.

Then King Midas said, " At last I feel
Eternity conquered beneath my heel

Like the glittering snake of Paradise—
And you are my Eve! "—but the maiden flies,

Like the leaping goat-footed waterfalls
Singing their cold, forlorn madrigals.

3.—CACOPHONY FOR CLARINET

SAID the dairymaid
With her hooped petticoat

Swishing like water . . .
To the hemlocks she said, " Afraid
Am I of each sheep and goat—
For I am Pan's daughter! "
Dark as Africa and Asia
The vast trees weep—
The Margravine learned as Aspasia,
Has fallen asleep.
Her small head, beribboned
With her yellow satin hair,
Like satin ribbons, butter-yellow,
That the faunal noon has made more mellow
Has drooped asleep . . .
And a snore forlorn
Sounds like Pan's horn.
On pointed toe I creep—
Look through the diamonded pane
Of the window in the dairy—
Then out I slip again,
In my hooped petticoat like old Morgane the fairy.
Like a still-room maid's yellow print gown
Are the glazed chintz buttercups of summer
Where the kingly cock in a feathered smock and a red-
gold crown
Rants like a barn-door mummer.
And I heard the Margravine say
To the ancient bewigged Abbé
" I think it is so clever
Of people to discover
New planets—and how ever
Do they find out what their names are? "
Then, clear as the note of a clarinet, her hair
Called Pan across the fields, Pan like the forlorn wind,

From the Asian, African darkness of the trees in his
 lair—
To play with her endless vacancy of mind!

4.—THE FOX

FOR ANN PEARN

Said old Sir Jason, the red-gold fox:
" The gardeners asleep, I will pick the locks:
His smooth leaves murmur like dark green seas,—
I will run beneath his nectarine trees.
But when it is dawn and the reynard-hued Sun
Will run through the tall empty town of the corn
And on my Gold Fleece gold spangles are born
Of the jangling dew,
Where the old cock crew,
Like that long-fleeced fox the Sun I will run
And my jangling gown
Will leave that tall town
With a rank and dank ragged-robin smell.
There is none to listen and none to tell,
As I tumble the old King toppling down.
For only my vixen wife will hark
Where the leaves of the wood are glittering dark
As the armoured men the King saw grow
From the earth ten thousand years ago.
When the kingly cock
In his feathered smock
With that five-hinged sword of wood, his crow,
Through the forest thrusts, I'll overthrow
This ancient King in his red-gold crown;
For now he is only a country clown

And his smock is a rustic long night-gown,
And a five-hinged sword of wood will not
Awaken a world that has fallen to rot
A world that's afraid
And pretends to be dead—
'Neath the wall of the tall nodding town of the shade.

5.—ROSE

(Imitated from Skelton)

In the fields like an Indian mazery
That the foolish moon has flowered,
Rose Bertin is walking lazily where
The fringe of the field is bowered

With trees as dark as the ancient creeds
Of China and of Ind . . .
Rose Bertin walks through the fields' pearled weeds
Where haunts the satyr wind.

" Where are you going to, my pretty maid,"
That negroid satyr sighs . . .
" To feed my pretty chucks, sir," she said—
" Each feathered thing that flies.

To feed them with the sun's gold grains
In the field's sparse Indian chintz;
But now those grains are spilt like rains,
And still light feathery glints

Fly in my brain." . . . Those bright birds flock,
The butterbump, the urban
Ranee stork, the turkey-cock
(Red paladin in a turban),

The crane who talks through his long nose,
The plump and foolish quail—
In their feather robes they follow Rose,
And never once they fail.

And Harriet, Susan, Rose and Polly,
Silken and frilled as a pigeon
Sleek them and praise the golden folly
That made laughing Rose a religion.

6.—POPULAR SONG

FOR CONSTANT LAMBERT

LILY O'GRADY,
Silly and shady,
Longing to be
A lazy lady,
Walked by the cupolas, gables in the
Lake's Georgian stables,
In a fairy tale like the heat intense,
And the mist in the woods when across the fence
The children gathering strawberries
Are changed by the heat into negresses,
Though their fair hair
Shines there
Like gold-haired planets, Calliope, Io,
Pomona, Antiope, Echo, and Clio.
Then Lily O'Grady,
Silly and shady,
Sauntered along like a
Lazy lady;
Beside the waves' haycocks her gown with tucks
Was of satin the colour of shining green ducks,

And her fol-de-rol
Parasol
Was a great gold sun o'er the haycocks shining,
But she was a negress black as the shade
That time on the brightest lady laid.
Then a satyr, dog-haired as trunks of trees,
Began to flatter, began to tease,
And she ran like the nymphs with golden foot
That trampled the strawberry, buttercup root,
In the thick gold dew as bright as the mesh
Of dead Panöpe's golden flesh,
Made from the music whence were born
Memphis and Thebes in the first hot morn,
—And ran, to wake
In the lake,
Where the water-ripples seem hay to rake.
And Charlottine,
Adeline,
Round rose-bubbling Victorine,
And the other fish
Express a wish
For mastic mantles and gowns with a swish;
And bright and slight as the posies
Of buttercups and of roses,
And buds of the wild wood-lilies
They chase her, as frisky as fillies.
The red retriever-haired satyr
Can whine and tease her and flatter,
But Lily O'Grady,
Silly and shady,
In the deep shade is a lazy lady;
Now Pompey's dead, Homer's read,
Heliogabalus lost his head,

And shade is on the brightest wing,
And dust forbids the bird to sing.

7.—THE FIVE MUSICIANS

The blue-leaved fig-trees swell with laughter,
Gold fissures split the ripe fruits after,

And like a gold-barred tiger, shade
Leaps in the darkness that they made.

The long-ribbed leaves shed light that dapples
Silenus like a tun of apples;

Gold-freckled, fruit-shaped faces stare
At nymphs with bodies white as air.

The ancient house rocked emptily
" Horned brothers, creep inside and see

Through my tall windows: the abode
Of noise is on the dusty road."

They creep . . . strange hands are on the hasp . . .
Silenus, sleepy as a wasp,

Amid the fruit-ripe heat, as in
An apricot or nectarine,

Replies, " The dust is wise and old . . .
For glistening fruits and Ophir's gold

Are gathered there to wake again
In our flesh, like a tune's refrain."

The five musicians with their bray
Shatter the fruit-ripe heat of day;

Their faces, wrinkled, kind, and old,
Are masked by the hot sun with gold;

Like fountains of blue water, gush
Their beards. Strange-feathered birds that hush,

Their song, move not so proud as these
Smiles floating, ageless courtesies.

They stand upon the dust outside;
Their tunes like drops of water died.

Yet still we hear their slow refrain,
" King Pharaoh, gay lad, come again! "

Miss Nettybun, beneath the tree,
Perceives that it is time for tea

And takes the child, a muslined moon,
Through the lustrous leaves of afternoon.

And tea-time comes with strawberry
Jam—yet where, oh *where*, is she?

On that music floating, gone
To China and to Babylon;

Never again she'll go to bed
In the sleepy house of Sir Rotherham Redde!

8.—SPRINGING JACK

GREEN wooden leaves clap light away
From the young flowers as white as day,—

Clear angel-face on hairy stalk;
(Soul grown from flesh, an ape's young talk.)

The showman's face is cubed, clear as
The shapes reflected in a glass,

Of water—(Glog, glut, a ghost's speech
Fumbling for space from each to each.)

The fusty showman fumbles, must
Fit in a particle of dust

The universe, for fear it gain
Its freedom from my box of brain.

Yet dust bears seeds that grow to grace
Behind my crude-striped wooden face,

As I, a puppet tinsel-pink
Leap on my spring, learn how to think;

Then like the trembling golden stalk
Of some long-petalled star, I walk

Through the dark heavens, until dew
Falls on my eyes and sense thrills through.

9.—THE HIGHER SENSUALISM

QUEEN CIRCE, the farmer's wife at the Fair,
Met three sailor-men stumping there,

Who came from the parrot-plumed sea, Yo-Ho!
And each his own trumpet began to blow.

" We come," said they, " from the Indian seas,
All bright as a parrot's feathers, and these

Break on gold sands of the perfumed isles,
Where the fruit is soft as a siren's smiles,

And the sun is as black as a Nubian.
We singed the beard of the King of Spain. . . .

Then we wandered once more on the South Sea strand
Where the icebergs seem Heavenly Mansions fanned

By the softest wind from the groves of spice,
And the angels like birds of paradise

Flit there: and we caught this queer-plumaged boy
(An angel, he calls himself) for a toy."

. . . . .

The Angel sighed: " Please, ma'am, if you'll spare
Me a trumpet, the angels will come to the Fair;

For even an angel must have his fling,
And ride on the roundabout, in the swing! "

She gave him a trumpet, but never a blare
Reached the angels from Midsummer Fair,

Though he played, " Will you hear a Spanish lady? "
And " Jack the Sailor," " Sweet Nelly," " Trees
shady "—

For only the gay hosannas of flowers
Sound, loud as brass bands, in those heavenly bowers.

Queen Circe said, " Young man, I will buy
Your plumaged coat for my pig to try—

Then with angels he'll go a-dancing hence
From sensuality into sense! "

The Fair's tunes like cherries and apricots
Ripened; the angels danced from their green grots;

Their hair was curled like the fruit on the trees . . .
Rigaudon, sarabande, danced they these.

And the pig points his toe and he curves his wings,
The music starts, and away he flings—

Dancing with angels all in a round,
Hornpipe and rigaudon on the Fair's ground.

10.—Polka

" ' Tra la la la—
See me dance the polka,'
Said Mr. Wagg like a bear,
' With my top hat
And my whiskers that—
(Tra la la la) trap the Fair.

Where the waves seem chiming haycocks
I dance the polka; there
Stand Venus' children in their gay frocks,—
Maroon and marine,—and stare

To see me fire my pistol
Through the distance blue as my coat;
Like Wellington, Byron, the Marquis of Bristol,
Buzbied great trees float.

While the wheezing hurdy-gurdy
Of the marine wind blows me
To the tune of Annie Rooney, sturdy,
Over the sheafs of the sea;

And bright as a seedsman's packet
With zinnias, candytufts chill,
Is Mrs. Marigold's jacket
As she gapes at the inn door still,

Where at dawn in the box of the sailor,
Blue as the decks of the sea,
Nelson awoke, crowed like the cocks,
Then back to the dust sank he.

And Robinson Crusoe
Rues so
The bright and foxy beer,—
But he finds fresh isles in a negress' smiles,—
(The poxy doxy dear,)

As they watch me dance the polka,'
Said Mr. Wagg like a bear,
' In my top hat and my whiskers that,—
Tra la la la, trap the Fair.

Tra la la la la—
Tra la la la la—
Tra la la la la la la la
La
La
La!' "

11.—KING COPHETUA AND THE BEGGAR MAID

THE five-pointed crude pink tinsel star
Laughed loudly at King Cophetua;

Across the plain that is black as mind
And limitless, it laughed unkind

To see him whitened like a clown
With the moon's flour, come in a golden crown.

The moon shone softer than a peach
Upon the round leaves in its reach;

The dark air sparkled like a sea—
The beggar-maid leaned out through a tree

And sighed (that pink flower-spike full of honey),
" Oh, for Love ragged as Time, with no money! "

Then through the black night the gardener's boy
As sunburnt as hay, came whispering, " Troy

Long ago was as sweet as the honey-chimes
In the flower-bells, jangling into rhymes,

And, oh, my heart's sweet as a honey-hive
Because of a wandering maid, and I live

But to tend the pale flower-bells of the skies
That shall drop down their dew on her sleeping eyes."

12.—SERENADE

THE tremulous gold of stars within your hair
Are yellow bees flown from the hive of night,
Finding the blossom of your eyes more fair
Than all the pale flowers folded from the light.
Then, Sweet, awake, and ope your dreaming eyes
Ere those bright bees have flown, and darkness dies.

13.—POOR MARTHA

BY white wool houses thick with sleep,
Wherein pig-snouted small winds creep,

With our white muslin faces clean,
We slip to see what can be seen.

Those rustling corn-sheaves the gold stars
Drop grain between the window-bars

Among dark leaves, all velvety—
(So seem the shadows) and we see

Crazed Martha tie up her brown hair
With the moon's blue ribbons, stare

At candles that are lit in vain—
They cannot penetrate her brain:

Their tinsel jargon seems to be
Incomprehensibility

To Martha's mind, though every word
Of hers they echo, like that bird

Of brilliant plumage, whose words please
The Indians by their bright-plumed seas.

The Fair's tunes bloom like myosotis,
Smooth-perfumèd stephanotis;

We children come with twisted curls
Like golden corn-sheaves, or fat pearls,

Like ondines in blue muslin dance
Around her; never once a glance

She gives us: " Can my love be true?
He promised he would bring me blue

Ribbons to tie up my brown hair.
He promised me both smooth and fair

That he would dive through brightest plumes
Of Indian seas for pearls, where glooms

The moon's blue ray; in her sleeping-chamber
Find me Thetis' fan of amber."

. . . . .

The candles preen and sleek their feathers . . .
" Pretty lady!" " Sweet June weathers."

But silence now lies all around
Poor Martha, since her love is drowned.

14.—COUNTRY COUSIN (*three variations*)

" A coral neck and a little song, so very extra, so very Susie."
GERTRUDE STEIN.

TO DOROTHY TODD

I

Perrine

IN summer when the rose-bushes
Have names like all the sweetest hushes
In a bird's song,—Susan, Hannah,
Martha, Harriet, and Rosannah,

Then round and flaxen blond leaves seem
Like country clouds of clouted cream,
And blossoms grow on trees above
As soft and thick as any dove.

The little girls go plucking sweet
Soft blooms with hands like coral feet
Of a piteous small sad bird
Upon a budding branch half heard,

While dew in trills, and dew in pearls,
Falls down upon their budding curls;
And ribbon blue as country streams,
Clear as a nightingale's song, dreams

Adown their frocks; each coral neck
Is sweet enough for birds to peck;
Their voices seem gold bells of corn,
The country winds pass by in scorn.

" How sweet," said Jeanne, " it would have been
If, when we reached our home, Perrine
Was there to greet us; golden grain
We'd give her, if she'd come again.

She was so faithful and so good,—
The humble hen we bought for food,
Then pitied, because she was lame
And was so trustful and so tame.

We nursed her back to health, and she
Became one of the family;
Of ragged robin was her bed,
Pink as her eyes; she laid her head

Down on this as she was bade;
Her crumpled crown looked limp and sad
And once she gave a little sigh,
But no complaint, when I was nigh.

And when for two weeks she had lain
There ill, she gained her strength again;
And then it seemed she found some beauty
In her humble lowly duty.

For each dawn, when through window-bars
Fade the straggling chickweed stars,
Perrine, forgetting her lame leg,
Would lay a sparkling golden egg.

For she had only this to give
And show her love; if those who live
With hopes of heaven ever gave
So much love, that, alone, could save

Our childish souls, made crystal clear,
And heaven itself would seem more dear.
But she is dead, our dear Perrine;
And if, tiptoe, we peep between

The thick leaves round the window bars,
Her eyes like pinkest campion stars
No more can peep at us, so kind
You'd think an angel swept her mind.

But if there is a heaven above
For hens who so must prove their love
I think that there, 'mid small wise flowers,
Perrine must pass the heavenly hours.

While there at last her five-point crown
Is gold, that crumpled, once lolled down! . . .
But now Perrine is dead, her fame
Is everywhere, though she was lame,—

And great kings come with golden crowns,
Sit by our leafy fire,—their towns
Deserting for Perrine's gold egg.
They try to buy it, steal it, beg. . . .

" Her beauty, white as any billow
Would wake King Canute from his pillow—
King Canute, lulled by his own snore,
Hearing the sound of wave no more

As he lies on a cloudy pillow
Beneath the weeping green willow."
So say the kings as they implore.
But dear Perrine lays eggs no more.

And in the briars of the cold wind
Where never rose blooms, hard, unkind,
I heard a pirate's voice that sighed:
(His face seemed the horizons wide)—

" I was a pirate, long ago;
But Time, if loaded with sweet snow
Of hawthorn, or with coral spray
Moves slowly, yet will die away.

Green honeycombs from flowers of limes,
The caverns, chiming sweet as rhymes
Along a flowery story seem;
We sailed by shores like some deep dream,

We sailed where every coral spray
Seemed like branches of pink may,
Fought Spanish ships whose patacoons
Seemed fireflies in the leafiest Junes.

But all these treasures I will leave,
And will not fret for them, or grieve,
If in these leafy lanes I find
An egg of Perrine good and kind."

Like housekeeping old hens that rustle
In a useful feather bustle,
From cottages, old women stoop—
Each cottage low as a hen-coop;

And the farmer and his old wife come
With candle-flames like a ripe plum.
" Why do your tears fall fast as rain,
When everything is all in vain? "

So now, by wintry hen-plumed seas,
In cackling grass the kings all freeze,—
The kings that their great castles leave
For dear Perrine . . . they weep and grieve

With gold crowns nodding in their dotage,
Where ragged flowers surround the cottage
(Perched upon a hen's thin legs).
Only the whining cold wind begs

Round each old king's long chequered dress,
And all the rest is nothingness.
Yet still our tears fall fast as rains ! . . .
But oh, the treasure Heaven gains.

II

Song

In summer when the rose-bushes
Have names like all the sweetest hushes
In a bird's song,—Susan, Hannah,
Martha, Harriet, and Rosannah,
My coral neck
And my little song
Are very extra
And very Susie;
A little kiss like a gold bee stings

My childish life so sweet and rosy . . .
Like country clouds of clouted cream
The round and flaxen blond leaves seem,
And dew in trills
And dew in pearls
Falls from every gardener's posy;
Marguerites, roses,
A flaxen lily,
Water-chilly,
Buttercups where the dew reposes—
In fact each flower young and silly,
The gardener ties in childish posies.

III

Song

THE clouds are bunchèd roses,
And the bunches seem
As thick as cream,
The country dozes and I dream.
" In a gown like a cauliflower.
My country cousin is—"
So said Susie
And her sister Liz.
Blossoms hang on trees above,
Soft and thick as any dove,
They mock my love;
Yet I pluck those feathers sweet
With my cold coral hands so like the
Small cold feet
Of a little sad bird,
On a budding branch heard.

15.—THREE POOR WITCHES

FOR W. T. WALTON

WHIRRING, walking
On the tree-top,
Three poor witches
Mow and mop.
Three poor witches
Fly on switches
Of a broom,
From their cottage room.
Like goat's beard rivers,
Black and lean,
Are Moll and Meg,
And Myrrhaline.
" Of those whirring witches, Meg "
(Bird-voiced fire screams)
" Has one leg;
Moll has two, on tree-tops see,
Goat-foot Myrrhaline has three ! "
When she walks
Turned to a wreath
Is every hedge;
She walks beneath
Flowered trees like water
Splashing down;
Her rich and dark silk
Plumcake gown
Has folds so stiff.
It stands alone
Within the fields
When she is gone.

And when she walks
Upon the ground
You'd never know
How she can bound
Upon the tree-tops, for she creeps
With a snail's slow silver pace;
Her milky silky wrinkled face
Shows no sign of her disgrace.
But walking on each
Leafy tree-top,—
Those old witches,
See them hop!
Across the blue-leaved
Mulberry tree
Of the rustling
Bunchèd sea,
To China, thick trees whence there floats
From wrens' and finches' feathered throats
Songs. The North Pole is a tree
With thickest chestnut flowers. . . We see
Them whizz and turn
Through Lisbon, churn
The butter-pats to coins gold,
Sheep's milk to muslin, thin and cold.
Then one on one leg,
One on two,
One on three legs
Home they flew
To their cottage; there one sees
And hears no sound but wind in trees;
One candle spills out thick gold coins
Where quilted dark with tree shade joins.

16.—PAVANE

ANNUNCIATA stands
On the flat lands
Under the pear-tree
(Jangling sweetly). See,
The curé-black leaves
Are cawing like a rook . . .
Annunciata grieves,
" No young man will look
At me with my harsh jangling hair
Pink as the one pear
(A flapping crude fish tinsel-pink
Flapping across the consciousness
Like laughter) and my tattered dress."
Then from the brink
Of the deep well,
Sounding like a bell,
From the castles under water
The old men seek the beggar's daughter . . .
Some were wrinkled grey
From suicide grown gay
And smiling, some were seen
With ivy limbs green
And gnarled with the water . . .
" Dance a pavane, beggar's daughter " . . .
They wooed her with book
And the water's tuneless bell
Wooed her as well—
A water-hidden sound achieves;
And cawing like a rook
Were the curé-black leaves . . .
One feather-breast of dew was grey

Upon round leaves—they fled away.
Only a moaning sound
From the castles that lie drowned
Beneath the fruit-boughs of the water
Reached the beggar's daughter.

17.—WHEN THE SAILOR

WHEN the sailor left the seas
They swayed like June's thick-leavèd trees;

The winds seemed only nightingales
That sang so sweetly leafy tales

Of rustic vows among deep leaves,—
Of Thisbe's love, how Priam grieves.

The sailor stumps his wooden leg
In shady lanes where he must beg,

Till skies shone like the fields he knew,—
Golden with buttercups and dew;

Then, slightly drunk, he sees an Inn
Beckon him to step within.

The parlour runs on feathered feet
Bird-like, " Neptune, thee we greet,"

It cries; the flames, an albatross,
Float on blue air like waves that toss,

Bird-like shriek, " The sea floats still
Just above the window-sill! "

" No, it is June's thick blue trees."
Heeding not the sound of these

Across the bar, through silver spray
Of the sweet and blossomed may,

Leaned the Circean landlady,
With her dark locks leafy shady,

And eyes that seemed the dancing sound
Of waves upon enchanted ground.

" Did you batter down Troy's wall,—
(Silver hawthorn trees grown tall),

Did you beg the Khan for mercy,
Did you meet the lady Circe? "

" She is changing like the sea . . .
Shadow, like a lovely lady

With an elegant footfall,
Never seemed so lovely; all

Her airs were beautiful as sleep,
Or dew too fair for flower to weep."

18.—FLEECING TIME

QUEEN VENUS, like a bunch of roses,
Fat and pink, that splashed dew closes,

Underneath dark mulberry trees,
Wandered with the fair-haired breeze.

Among the dark leaves, preening wings,
Sit golden birds of light; each sings,

" Will you accept the blue muslin? "
As they peck the blackamoor mulberries' skin.

Then came a sheep like a sparkling cloud;
" Oh, ma'am, please, ma'am, sleek me proud,

Come fleece and comb my golden wool
And do not mind, ma'am, if you pull! "

Her flocks came thick as the mulberries
That grow on the dark, clear mulberry trees,

As thick as the daisies in the sky . . .
Prince Paris, Adonis; as each passed by

She cried, " Come feed on buds as cold
As my fleeced lamb-tailed river's gold,

And you shall dance like each golden bird
Of light that sings in dark trees unheard,

And you shall skip like my lamb-tailed river,
In my buttercup fields for ever."

The lady Venus, with hair thick as wool,
Cried " Come and be fleeced—each sheepish fool! "

19.—EVENING

Prince Absolam and Sir Rotherham Redde
Rode on a rocking-horse home to bed,

With dreams like cherries ripening big
Beneath the frondage of each wig.

In a flat field on the road to Sleep
They ride together, a-hunting sheep

That like the swan-bright fountains seem;
Their tails hang down as meek as a dream.

Prince Absolam seems a long-fleeced bush,
The heat's tabernacle, in the hush

And the glamour of eve, when buds the dew
Into bright tales that never come true;

And as he passes a cherry-tree
Caught by his long hair, bound is he,

While all his gold fleece flows like water
Into the lap of Sir Rotherham's daughter.

Come then, and sit upon the grass
With cherries to pelt you, as bright as glass—

Vermilion bells that sound as clear
As the bright swans whose sighing you hear

When they float to their crystal death
Of water, scarcely plumed by the breath

Of air—so clear in the round leaves
They look, this crystal sound scarce grieves,

As they pelt down like tears fall'n bright
From music or some deep delight.

The gardener cut off his beard of bast
And tied up the fountain-tree, made it fast

And bound it together till who could see
Which is Prince Absolam, which is the tree?

Only his gold fleece flows like water
Into the lap of Sir Rotherham's daughter;

Sir Rotherham Redde gathers bags of gold
Instead of the cherries ruddy and cold.

20.—ON THE VANITY OF HUMAN ASPIRATIONS

"In the time of King James I, the aged Countess of Desmond met her death, at the age of a hundred and forty years, through falling from an apple-tree."—*Chronicles of the times.*

In the cold wind, towers grind round,
Turning, turning, on the ground;

In among the plains of corn
Each tower seems a unicorn.

Beneath a sad umbrageous tree
Anne, the goose-girl, could I see—

But the umbrageous tree behind
Ne'er cast a shadow on her mind—

A goose-round breast she had, goose-brains,
And a nose longer than a crane's;

A clarinet sound, cold, forlorn,
Her harsh hair, straight as yellow corn,

And her eyes were round, inane
As the blue pebbles of the rain.

Young Anne, the goose-girl, said to me,
" There's been a sad catastrophe!

The aged Countess still could walk
At a hundred and forty years, could talk,

And every eve in the crystal cool
Would walk by the side of the clear fish-pool.

But to-day when the Countess took her walk
Beneath the apple-trees, from their stalk

The apples fell like the red-gold crown
Of those kings that the Countess had lived down,

And they fell into the crystal pool;
The grandmother fish enjoying the cool—

(Like the bright queens dyed on a playing-card
They seemed as they fanned themselves, flat and
hard)—

Floated in long and chequered gowns
And darting, searched for the red-gold crowns

In the Castles drownèd long ago
Where the empty years pass weedy-slow,

And the water is flat as equality
That reigns over all in the heavenly

State we aspire to, where none can choose
Which is the goose-girl, which is the goose.—

But the Countess climbed up the apple-tree,
Only to see what she could see—

Because to persons of her rank
The usual standpoint is that of the bank! . . ."

The goose-girl smoothed down her feather-soft
Breast . . . " When the Countess came aloft,

King James and his courtiers, dressed in smocks,
Rode by a-hunting the red-gold fox,

And King James, who was giving the view-halloo
Across the corn, too loudly blew,

And the next that happened was—what did I see
But the Countess fall'n from the family tree!

Yet King James could only see it was naughty
To aspire to the high at a hundred and forty,

' Though if ' (as he said) ' she aspired to climb
To Heaven—she certainly has, this time! ' "

. . . And Anne, the goose-girl, laughed, " Tee-hee,
It was a sad catastrophe! "

21.—GREEN GEESE

FOR RICHARD JENNINGS

THE trees were hissing like green geese . . .
The words they tried to say were these:

" When the great Queen Claude was dead
They buried her deep in the potting-shed."

The moon smelt sweet as nutmeg-root
On the ripe peach-trees' leaves and fruit,

And her sandal-wood body leans upright,
To the gardener's fright, through the summer night.

. . . . .

The bee-wing'd warm afternoon light roves
Gilding her hair (wooden nutmegs and cloves),

And the gardener plants his seedsman's samples
Where no wild unicorn herd tramples—

In clouds like potting-sheds he pots
The budding planets in leaves cool as grots,

For the great Queen Claude when the light's gilded
gaud
Sings Miserere, Gloria, Laud.

But when he passes the potting-shed,
Fawning upon him comes the dead—

Each cupboard's wooden skeleton
Is a towel-horse when the clock strikes one,

And light is high—yet with ghosts it winces
All night 'mid wrinkled tarnished quinces,

When the dark air seems soft down
Of the wandering owl brown.

They know the clock-faced sun and moon
Must wrinkle like the quinces soon

(That once in dark blue grass dew-dabbled
Lay) . . . those ghosts like turkeys gabbled

To the scullion baking the Castle bread—
" The Spirit, too, must be fed, be fed;

Without our flesh we cannot see—
Oh, give us back Stupidity! " . . .

But death had twisted their thin speech
It could not fit the mind's small niche—

Upon the warm blue grass outside,
They realized that they had died.

Only the light from their wooden curls roves
Like the sweet smell of nutmegs and cloves

Buried deep in the potting-shed,
Sighed those green geese, " Now the Queen is dead."

22.—TWO KITCHEN SONGS

I

The harsh bray and hollow
Of the pot and the pan
Seems Midas defying
The great god Apollo!
The leaves' great golden crowns
Hang on the trees;
The maids in their long gowns
Hunt me through these.
Grand'am, Grand'am,
From the pan I am
Flying . . . country gentlemen
Took flying Psyche for a hen
And aimed at her; then turned a gun
On harmless chicken-me—for fun.
The beggars' dogs howl all together,
Their tails turn to a ragged feather;
Pools, like mirrors hung in garrets,
Show each face as red as a parrot's,
Whistling hair that raises ire
In cocks and hens in the kitchen fire!
Every flame shrieks cockle-doo-doo
(With their cockscombs flaring high too);
The witch's rag-rug takes its flight
Beneath the willows' watery light:
The wells of water seem a-plume—
The old witch sweeps them with her broom—
All are chasing chicken-me. . . .
But Psyche—where, oh where, is she?

II

GREY as a guinea-fowl is the rain
Squawking down from the boughs again.
" Anne, Anne,
Go fill the pail,"
Said the old witch who sat on the rail.
" Though there is a hole in the bucket,
Anne, Anne,
It will fill my pocket;
The water-drops when they cross my doors
Will turn to guineas and gold moidores. . . ."
The well-water hops across the floors;
Whimpering, " Anne " it cries, implores,
And the guinea-fowl-plumaged rain,
Squawking down from the boughs again,
Cried, " Anne, Anne, go fill the bucket,
There is a hole in the witch's pocket—
And the water-drops like gold moidores,
Obedient girl, will surely be yours.
So, Anne, Anne,
Go fill the pail
Of the old witch who sits on the rail! "

23.—SPINNING SONG

THE miller's daughter
Combs her hair,
Like flocks of doves
As soft as vair . . .

Oh, how those soft flocks flutter down
Over the empty grassy town.

Like a queen in a crown
Of gold light, she
Sits 'neath the shadows'
Flickering tree—

Till the old dame went the way she came,
Playing bobcherry with a candle-flame.

Now Min the cat
With her white velvet gloves
Watches where sat
The mouse with her loves—

(Old and malicious Mrs. Grundy
Whose washing-day is from Monday to Monday.)

" Not a crumb," said Min,
" To a mouse I'll be giving,
For a mouse must spin
To earn her living."

So poor Mrs. Mouse and her three cross Aunts
Nibble snow that rustles like gold wheat plants.

And the miller's daughter
Combs her locks,
Like running water
Those dove-soft flocks;

And her mouth is sweet as a honey-flower cold
But her heart is heavy as bags of gold.

The shadow-mice said
" We will line with down
From those doves, our bed
And our slippers and gown,

For everything comes to the shadows at last
If the spinning-wheel Time move slow or fast."

24.—THE BEAR

WATER-GREEN is the flowing pollard
In Drowsytown; a smocked dullard
Sits upon the noodle
Soft and milky grass,—
Clownish-white was that fopdoodle
As he watched the brown bear pass . . .
" Who speaks of Alexander
And General Hercules,
And who speaks of Lysander?
For I am strong as these!
The housekeeper's old rug
Is shabby brown as me,
And if I wished to hug
Those heroes, they would flee,—
For always when I show affection
They take the contrary direction.
I passed the barrack square
In nodding Drowsytown,—
Where four-and-twenty soldiers stare
Through slits of windows at the Bear,"
(So he told the Clown.)
" Twelve were black as Night the Zambo,
(Black shades playing at dumb crambo!)

Twelve were gilded as the light,
Goggling negro eyes of fright.
There they stood, and each mentero,
Striped and pointed, leaned to Zero . . .
Grumbling footsteps of the Bear,
Came near . . . they did fade in air,
The window shut and they were gone
The Brown Bear lumbered on alone."
So he told the smocked fopdoodle,
White and flapping as the air,
Sprawling on the grass for pillow—
(Milky soft as any noodle)
'Neath the water-green willow
There in Drowsytown
Where one crumpled cottage nods—
Nodding
Nodding
Down.

25.—WHY

NOAH's granddaughter
Sat on his knee;
Her questions like water
Gushed ceaselessly.

Her hair's gilded wool
Seems the sun's tent;
Her mouth, a grape golden-cool,
Shows through the rent.

Noah's replies
Are all one hears;
And the small ripples rise
Like listening ass-ears.

“ That young giraffe?
His proud elevation
Raises a laugh
To the height of quotation. . . .

The camel’s face
Is like Mrs. Grundy’s;
He makes that grimace
At working on Sundays.

The kangaroo, chaste,
Of Victorian complexion,
Wears at her waist
Each pledge of affection.

The trunk of the elephant
Is not a box,
The cock’s gilded crown can’t
Frighten the fox.”

. . . . .

The sea-gods talk Greek . . .
But they learn the word “ why ”;
Like leaves of the palm,
Their beards, gilded and dry

Are spreading upon
The blue marble Pompeii
Whose temples are gone
(So the sea seems); Aglae

Asks “ What for? ” . . . The waves’ door
Begins to slam.
Like water the questions pour.
Noah said “ Damn ! ”

26.—EN FAMILLE

In the early spring-time, after their tea,
Through the young fields of the springing Bohea,
Jemima, Jocasta, Dinah, and Deb
Walked with their father, Sir Joshua Jebb,—
An admiral red, whose only notion,
(A butterfly poised on a pigtailed ocean)
Is of the peruked sea whose swell
Breaks on the flowerless rocks of Hell.
Under the thin trees, Deb and Dinah,
Jemima, Jocasta, walked, and finer
Their black hair seemed (flat-sleek to see)
Than the young leaves of the springing Bohea;
Their cheeks were like nutmeg-flowers when swells
The rain into foolish silver bells.
They said, " If the door you would only slam,
Or if, Papa, you would once say ' Damn '—
Instead of merely roaring ' Avast '
Or boldly invoking the nautical Blast—
We should now stand in the street of Hell
Watching siesta shutters that fell
With a noise like amber softly sliding;
Our moon-like glances through these gliding
Would see at her table preened and set
Myrrhina sitting at her toilette
With eyelids closed as soft as the breeze
That flows from gold flowers on the incense-trees."

. . . . .

The Admiral said, " You could never call—
I assure you it would not do at all!
She gets down from table without saying ' Please,'
Forgets her prayers and to cross her T's,

In short, her scandalous reputation
Has shocked the whole of the Hellish nation;
And every turbaned Chinoiserie,
With whom we should sip our black Bohea,
Would stretch out her simian fingers thin
To scratch you, my dears, like a mandoline;
For Hell is just as properly proper
As Greenwich, or as Bath, or Joppa! "

TWO PROMENADES SENTIMENTALES

I

RAIN

BESIDE the smooth black lacquer sea
You and I move aimlessly.

The grass is springing pale, alone,
Tuneless as a quartertone. . . .

Remote your face seems, far away
Beneath the ghostly water, Day,

That laps across you, rustling loud—
Until you seem a muslined cloud

Beneath your fluted hat's ghost-flowers—
The little dog that runs and cowers

Black as Beelzebub, now tries
To catch the white lace butterflies. . . .

But we are mute and move again
Across the wide and endless plain,

Vague as the little nachreous breeze
That plays with gilt rococo seas.

We are two ghosts to-day—each ghost
For ever wandering and lost;

No yesterday and no to-morrow
Know we—neither joy nor sorrow,

For this is the hour when like a swan
The silence floats, so still and wan,

That bird-songs, silver masks to hide
Strange faces, now all sounds have died,

Find but one curdled sheepskin flower
Embodied in this ghostly hour. . . .

II

THE PROFESSOR SPEAKS

One time when the cold red winter sun
Like a Punch and Judy show shrilled in fun

And scattered down its green perfume
Like the dust that drifts from the green lime-bloom,

I sat at my dressing-table—that chilly
Palely crinolined water-lily

And watched my face as spined and brittle
As the tall fish, tangled in a little

Dark weed, that sea-captains keep
In bottles and perpetual sleep.

My face seemed the King of Spain's dry map
All seamed with gold . . . no one cared a rap

As I walked on the grass, like the sheepish buds
Of wool that grow on lambs chewing their cuds.

The small flowers grew to a hairy husk
That holds Eternity for its musk

And the satyr's daughter came: I saw
She was golden as Venus' castle of straw,

And the curls round her golden fruit-face shine
Like black ivy-berries that will not make wine.

With my black cloak—(a three-tiered ship on the
main)
And my face like the map of the King of Spain,

Beneath the boughs where like ragged goose-plumes
Of the snow hang the spring's first chilly blooms,

I swept on towards her; my foot with the gout
Clattered like satyr-hoofs, put her to rout,

For she thought that I was the satyr-king . . .
So she fled like the goat-legged wind of spring

Across the sea that was green as grass,
Where bird-soft archipelagos pass—

To where like golden bouquets lay
Asia, Africa, and Cathay.

And now the bird-soft light and shade
Touches me not; I promenade

Where rain falls with tinkling notes, and cold,
Like the castanet-sound of the thinnest gold

In chessboard gardens where, knight and pawn
Of ivory, scentless flowers are born.

WINTER

To Veronica

Dagobert lay in front of the fire . . .
Each thin flame seemed a feathery spire

Of the grasses that like goslings quack
On the castle walls : " Bring Gargotte back " ;

But Gargotte the goose-girl, bright as hail,
Has faded into a fairy-tale.

The kings and queens on the nursery wall
Seem chain-armoured fish in the moat, and all

The frost-flowers upon the window-panes,
Grown fertilate from the fire's gold grains,

Ripen to gold-freckled strawberries,
Raspberries, glassy-pale gooseberries—

(We never could touch them, early or late,
They would chill our hands like the touch of Fate.)

But Anne was five years old and must know
Reality ; in the goose-soft snow

She was made to walk with her three tall aunts
Drooping beneath the snow's cold plants.

They dread the hour when with book and bell
Their mother, the old fell Countess of L——

Is disrobed of her wig and embalmed for the night's
Sweet mummified dark; her invective affrights

The maids till you hear them scamper like mice
In the wainscoting—trembling, neat and nice.

Each clustered bouquet of the snows is
Like stephanotis and white roses;

The muted airs sing Palestrina
In trees like monstrances, grown leaner

Than she is; the unripe snow falls
Like little tunes on the virginals

Whose sound is bright, unripe and sour
As small fruits fall'n before their hour.

The Countess sits and plays fantan
Beneath the portrait of great Queen Anne

(Who sleeps beneath the strawberry bed);
And all her maids have scampered, fled.

The shuffled cards like the tail of a bird
Unfolding its shining plumes are heard. . . .

The maid in her powder-closet soon
Beneath the fire of the calm full moon

Whose sparkles, rubies, sapphires, spill
For her upon the window-sill

Will nod her head, grown sleepy, I wis,
As Alaciel, or Semiramis,

Pasiphae, or the lady Isis,
Embalmed in the precious airs like spices.

But her ladyship stamps with her stick . . . " Grown
cold
Are my small feet, from my chilly gold—

Unwarmed by buds of the lamb's wool . . . go
And gather for me the soft polar snow

To line with that silver chilly-sweet
The little slippers upon my feet—

With snow clear-petalled as lemon blossom—
Crystal-clear—perfumed as Venus' bosom."

. . . . .

Can this be Eternity?—snow peach-cold,
Sleeping and rising and growing old,

While she lies embalmed in the fire's gold sheen,
Like a cross wasp in a ripe nectarine,

And the golden seed of the fire droops dead
And ripens not in the heart or head!

HERODIADE

To Inez Chandos-Pole

The snow dies, that was cold as coral,
Or a fairy-story's moral,

And birds put forth their song's soft flowers
In the thickets and the bowers.

Salome walks the lands . . . the quaint
Flowers crisp as snow, and youthful, feint

To watch from Heaven's palaces,
With footsteps soft as calices

The angels come as pages, show
Salome how to touch the low

Lute-notes and dance the sarabande,
Leading the Princess by the hand,

Until Salome's nurse appears,
Harsh as the snow; with shivering fears

The angels go again, discern
Theirs is no dance that she must learn.

NIGHT PIECE

The shadows' saracenic hordes
Overcome sweet firelight's lauds
That still seem flowering as they pray
To pictured kings that fade away.
The flickering firelight whispered " Hush! "
Flowering like a pale rose-bush,
To kings and queens in coats of mail
Melting like the first spring hail.
The cold night seems like wintry boughs,—
Calm as a nightingale's song grows
The old forgetful wind outside
That faded to a whisper, died.

. . . . .

Now shadows seem the wives, grown dim,
Of Algalath, Galgalath, Saraim,
Those negro kings . . . each nods her head
And walks through doors that lead to bed,
Nodding their dark heads adown.
Outside, leaves like a starry crown
Are clear as the splintered star ice-green
That is a crown for a negro queen.
Downstairs the household noises die,
The water seems a lullaby,
And soft snow sings among the leaves
Upon the boughs and castle eaves.

And only the fire's drowsy glow
Upon the soft bird-throats of snow

Made those feathers bull-finch soft
And rosy, singing from the loft.
And the shadows, negro queens, (grown dim)
Of Algalath, Galgalath, Saraim,
Nod their heads in the halcyon clime
Of age and wait for the clock's cold chime.

BY THE LAKE

Across the thick and the pastel snow
Two people go. . . . " And do you remember
When last we wandered this shore ? " . . . " Ah no !
For it is cold-hearted December."
" Dead, the leaves that like asses' ears hung on the trees
When last we wandered and squandered joy here ;
Now Midas your husband will listen for these
Whispers—these tears for joy's bier."
And as they walk, they seem tall pagodas ;
And all the ropes let down from the cloud
Ring the hard cold bell-buds upon the trees—codas
Of overtones, ecstasies, grown for love's shroud.

PRELUDE

For Geoffrey Gorer

When our long sun into the dark had set
And made but winter branches of his rays—
I left my heart.
So doth a shadow leave
The body when our long dark sun is gone.

Now the black chaos of the Polar night
Melts in the hearts of the forgotten Dead;—
The tears turned ice about each loveless head
Are changed into bird-plumaged bird-voiced springs
And the sap rises like a bird that sings.

The cold wind creaking in my plant-shrill blood
Seems spring beginning in some earthen bud
Though immemorial, the winter's shade
Furred my cold blood wherein plant, beast, are laid,
In that dark earth from which shall spring the soul

As dark and broken hints of sciences
Forgotten, and strange satyrine alliances
Of beast and soul lie hidden in the old
Immensity and desert of the cold.

Hoarse as a dog's bark the furled heavy leaves
Are hairy as a dog: furred fire barks for the shape
Of hoarse-voiced animals; cold air agape
Whines to be shut in the water's shape and plumes;
All things break from the imprisoning winter's glooms;

All things, all hearts awake—
Until the gold within the miser's heart
Would buy the siren isles and many a chart
From dream to dream, and the death-blinded eyes
See beyond wild bird-winged discoveries.

All creatures praise the sun in their degree:
The mother bear with thick forestial fur
And grumbling footsteps, lumbering primal sleep
Of the winter earth, as furry as a bear
And grumbling deep,
No longer sees her cubs as a black blot
As clots of thick black darkness; primal form
Is shaped from that thick night—
Begins from this black chaos: life is light.

The stunted long-armed gardener mossed as trees
Has known before his birth—
For he was born and shaped close to the earth—
Best of all things are water, and hot gold
Of the rough fruitful sun: best of all things are these.
So the slow gold of his hot days and rays
Ripened within our earth and changed to fruits,
So the cold twisted water changed to roots
Of apple-trees.

But I, a harpy like a nightingale,
A nightingale that seems a harpy, mourn
With my heart changed now from a black blind stone
That rolls down the abyss, to a ghost gone
Or a black shadow cast
Upon the dust where gossips of mean Death—
The small and gilded scholars of the Fly

That feed upon the crowds and their dead breath
Still buzz and stink where the bright heroes die
Of the dust's rumours and the old world's fevers.
Sometimes in the arena like a drum
My heart sounds, calls the heroes from their shade
Till with the march of tides, those tall ghosts come
Where Fortune, Virtue, Folly, Wisdom, these—
Mimes garbed as aeons, by horizons bound—
With monstrous trumpetings of suns at war
Amid earth-quaking rumour of crowds whispering
And bull-voiced bellowings of tropic light
Contend . . .
And the huge bulk of Folly fell
From her world-height in the arena. Hell
Has dyed its fires upon the fairest faces
And where the hero smiled, bare Death grimaces.
But one who changed the complexion of all nights,
Whose lips have fired Persepolis, to me
Spoke then of eagle-winged Icarian flights
Of the steel men across an ageless sea,
And continents and quays where the one nation
Of the blind smiling statues still abide
Beneath giant suns whose sound no man hath known.
And huge horizons and the enchanted tide,
The azure unattainable and wide,
These they have known, and in their marble veins
Are all the summer sorrow of the rose,
And siren waves.
In the agonic noon
When the black pyres and pyramids of shade
Are mute as solemn and revengeful ghosts
Left from the tombs of night, I, a ghost laid,
Walk like a ghost among the city ways,

Pressed on by hungry continents of stone.
Yet still the light brings life to those unborn
And still the statues hear the sirens' song
Across the deep-boughed gardens of the sea.

Where the first founts and the deep waterways
Of the young light flow down and lie like peace
Upon the upturned faces of the blind,
The crooked has a shadow light makes straight,
The shallow places gain their depth again,
It comes to bless;
And man-made chasms between man and man
Of creeds and tongues are filled.
The guiltless light
Remakes all things and men in holiness.

Note.—The third line in the second stanza is an echo of a line from Dante. The fourth line in the eighth stanza a rough translation from a line in a Pindar.

MARINE

I.—FIREWORKS

PINK faces—(worlds or flowers or seas or stars),
You all alike are patterned with hot bars

Of coloured light; and falling where I stand,
The sharp and rainbow splinters from the band

Seem fireworks, splinters of the Infinite—
(Glitter of leaves the echoes). And the night

Will weld this dust of bright Infinity
To forms that we may touch and call and see:

Pink pyramids of faces: tulip-trees
Spilling night-perfumes on the terraces.

The music, blond airs waving like a sea
Draws in its vortex of immensity

The new-awakened flower-strange hair and eyes
Of crowds beneath the floating summer skies.

And, 'gainst the silk pavilions of the sea
I watch the people move incessantly

Vibrating, petals blown from flower-hued stars
Beneath the music-fireworks' waving bars;

So all seems indivisible, at one:
The flow of hair, the flowers, the seas that run,—

A coloured floating music of the night
Through the pavilions of the Infinite.

2.—MINSTRELS

Beside the sea, metallic bright
And sequined with the noisy light,
Duennas slowly promenade
Each like a patch of sudden shade,

While colours like a parokeet
Shrill loudly to the chattering heat;
And gowns as white as innocence
With sudden sweetness take the sense.

Those crested paladins the waves
Are sighing to their tawny slaves
The sands, where, orange-turban'd stand—
Opaque black gems—the negro band!

While in the purring greenery
The crowd moves like a tropic sea—
The people, sparkles from the heat
That dies from ennui at our feet.

The instruments that snore like flies
Seem mourners at Time's obsequies.
The sun, a pulse's beat, inflates
And with the band coagulates:

" A thousand years seem but a day—
Time waits for no man, yet he'll stay
Bewildered when we cross this bar
Into the Unknown—there we are!

Eternity and Time commence
To merge amid the somnolence
Of winding circles, bend on bend,
With no beginning and no end,

Down which they chase queer tunes that gape
Till they come close,—then just escape!
But though Time's barriers are defied
They never seem quite satisfied.

The crowds, bright sparks struck out by Time,
Pass, touch each other, never chime:
Each soul a separate entity—
Some past, some present, some to be:

But now, an empty blot of white,
Beneath the senseless shocks of light
Flashed by the tunes that cannot thrill
The nerves. Oh! Time is hard to kill!

3.—PEDAGOGUES

THE air is like a jarring bell
That jangles words it cannot spell,
And black as Fate, the iron trees
Stretch thirstily to catch the breeze.

The fat leaves pat the shrinking air;
The hot sun's patronizing stare
Rouses the stout flies from content
To some small show of sentiment.

Beneath the terrace shines the green
Metallic strip of sea, and sheen
Of sands, where folk flaunt parrot-bright
With rags and tags of noisy light.

The brass band's snorting stabs the sky
And tears the yielding vacancy—
The imbecile and smiling blue
Until fresh meaning trickles through;

And slowly we perambulate
With spectacles that concentrate,
In one short hour, Eternity,
In one small lens, Infinity.

With children, our primeval curse,
We overrun the universe—
Beneath the giddy lights of noon,
White as a tired August moon.

The air is like a jarring bell
That jangles words it cannot spell,
And black as Fate, the iron trees
Stretch thirstily to catch the breeze.

4.—SWITCHBACK

By the blue wooden sea,
Curling laboriously,

Coral and amber grots
(Cherries and apricots),
Ribbons of noisy heat,
Binding them head and feet,
Horses as fat as plums
Snort as each bumpkin comes:
Giggles like towers of glass
(Pink and blue spirals) pass;
Oh, how the Vacancy
Laughed at them rushing by!
" Turn again, flesh and brain,
Only yourselves again!
How far above the Ape,
Differing in each shape,
You with your regular,
Meaningless circles are! "

5.—MYSELF ON THE MERRY-GO-ROUND

THE giddy sun's kaleidoscope,
The pivot of a switchback world,
Is tied to it by many a rope:
The people (flaunting streamers), furled
Metallic banners of the seas,
The giddy sun's kaleidoscope
Casts colours on the face of these:
Cosmetics of Eternity,
And powders faces blue as death;
Beneath the parasols we see
Gilt faces tarnished by sea-breath,
And crawling like the foam, each horse
Beside the silken tents of sea
In whirlpool circles takes his course.

Huge houses, humped like camels, chase
The wooden horses' ceaseless bound;
The throbbing whirring sun that drags
The streets upon its noisy round
With tramways chasing them in vain,
Projects in coloured cubes each face—
Then shatters them upon our brain.
The house-fronts hurl them back, they jar
Upon cross-currents of the noise:
Like atoms of my soul they are,
They shake my body's equipoise,—
A clothes line for the Muse to fly
(So thin and jarred and angular)
Her rags of tattered finery.
Beneath the heat the trees' sharp hue—
A ceaseless whirr, metallic-green—
Sounds like a gimlet shrilling through
The mind, to reach the dazzling sheen
Of meanings life can not decide:
Then words set all awry, and you
Are left upon the other side.
Our senses, each a wooden horse,
We paint till they appear to us
Like life, and then queer strangers course
In our place on each Pegasus.
The very heat seems but to be
The product of some man-made force—
Steam from the band's machinery.
The heat is in a thousand rags
Reverberant with sound, whose dry
Frayed ends we never catch, seem tags
Of our unfinished entity;
And like a stretched accordion

The houses throb with heat, and flags
Of smoke are tunes light plays upon.
The band's kaleidoscopic whirr
Tears up those jarring threads of heat,
The crowds: plush mantles seem to purr;
Crustacean silk gowns take the beat
From houses; each reverberates
With this vitality and stir
The giddy heat acerberates.
And in the swirling restaurant
Where liqueurs at perpetual feud
Dispute for sequined lights and taunt
Hot leaves, our dusty souls exude
Their sentiments, while scraps of sense
Float inward from the band and flaunt—
Disturb the general somnolence.

METROPOLITAN

I.—STOPPING PLACE

THE world grows furry, grunts with sleep . . .
But I must on the surface keep.
The jolting of the train to me
Seems some primeval vertebrae
Attached by life-nerves to my brain—
Grown primitive, till, once again,
I see all shapes as crude and new
And ordered,—with some end in view,
No longer with the horny eyes
Of other people's memories.
Through highly varnished yellow heat,
As through a lens that does not fit,
The faces jolt in cubes, and I
Perceive their odd solidity
Anchored against the puff of breeze,
As shallow as the crude blue seas ;
And there are woollen buns to eat—
Bright-varnished buns to touch and see
And, black as an Inferno, tea.
Then (Reckett's blue) a puff of wind . . .
Heredity regains my mind
And I am sitting in the train
While thought becomes like flesh,—the brain
A horny substance altering sight;
How strange, intangible is light
Whence all is born, and yet by touch
We live,—the rest is not worth much . . .

Once more the world grows furred with sleep,—
But I must on the surface keep
While mammoths from the heat are born—
Great clumsy trains with tusk and horn
Whereon the world's too sudden tossed
Through frondage of our mind, and lost.

2.—MISS NETTYBUN AND THE SATYR'S CHILD

As underneath the trees I pass
Through emerald shade on hot soft grass,
Petunia faces, glowing-hued
With heat, cast shadows hard and crude—
Green velvety as leaves, and small
Fine hairs like grass pierce through them all.
But these are all asleep—asleep,
As through the schoolroom door I creep
In search of you, for you evade
All the advances I have made.
Come, Horace, you must take my hand :
This sulking state I will not stand!
But you shall feed on strawberry jam
At tea-time, if you cease to slam
The doors that open from our sense—
Through which I slipped to drag you hence!

3.—PORTRAIT OF A BARMAID

METALLIC waves of people jar
Through crackling green toward the bar

Where on the tables, chattering-white
The sharp drinks quarrel with the light.

Those coloured muslin blinds the smiles
Shroud wooden faces in their wiles—

Sometimes they splash like water (you
Yourself reflected in their hue).

The conversation, loud and bright,
Seems spinal bars of shunting light

In firework-spirting greenery.
O complicate machinery

For building Babel, iron crane
Beneath your hair, that blue-ribbed mane

In noise and murder like the sea
Without its mutability!

Outside the bar, where jangling heat
Seems out of tune and off the beat,

A concertina's glycerine
Exudes and mirrors in the green

Your soul, pure glucose edged with hints
Of tentative and half-soiled tints.

4.—THE SPIDER

THE fat light clings upon my skin,
Like grease that slowly forms a thin
And foul white film ; so close it lies,
It feeds upon my lips and eyes.

The black fly hits the window-pane
That shuts its dirty body in;
So once, his spirit fought to quit
The body that imprisoned it.

He always seemed so fond of me,
Until one day he chanced to see
My head, a little on one side,
Loll softly as if I had died.

Since then, he rarely looked my way,
Though he could never know what lay
Within my brain; though iron his will,
I thought, he's young and teachable.

And often, as I took my drink,
I chuckled in my heart to think
Whose dark blood ran within his veins:
You see, it spared me half my pains.

The time was very long until
I had the chance to work my will;
Once seen, the way was clear as light,
A father's patience infinite.

He always was so sensitive;
But soon I taught him how to live
With each day, just a patch of white,
A blinded patch of black, each night.

Each day he watched my gaiety:
It's very difficult to die
When one is young . . . I pitied him,
The glass I filled up to the brim.

His shaking fingers scarce could hold;
His limbs were trembling as with cold . . .
I waited till from night and day
All meaning I had wiped away,

And then I gave it him again;
The wine made heaven in his brain:
Then spider-like, the kindly wine
Thrust tentacles through every vein,

And knotted him so very fast
I knew I had him safe at last.
And sometimes in the dawn, I'd creep
To watch him as he lay asleep,

And each time, see my son's face grown
In some blurred line, more like my own.
A crumpled rag, he lies all night
Until the first white smear of light;

And sleep is but an empty hole . . .
No place for him to hide his soul,
No outlet there to set him free:
He never can escape from me.

Yet still I never know what thought,
All fly-like, in his mind lies caught:
His face seems some half-spoken word
Forgot again as soon as heard

Beneath the livid skin of light;
Oh, just an empty space of white,
Now all the meaning's gone. I'll sit
A little while, and stare at it.

5.—THE DRUNKARD

THIS black tower drinks the blinding light.
Strange windows livid white,

Tremble beneath the curse of God.
Yet living weeds still nod

To the huge sun, a devil's eye
That tracks the souls that die.

The clock beats like the heart of Doom
Within the narrow room;

And whispering with some ghastly air
The curtains float and stir.

But still she never speaks a word;
I think she hardly heard

When I with reeling footsteps came
And softly spoke her name.

But yet she does not sleep. Her eyes
Still watch in wide surprise

The thirsty knife that pitied her;
But those lids never stir,

Though creeping Fear still gnaws like pain
The hollow of her brain.

She must have some sly plan, the cheat,
To lie so still. The beat

That once throbbed like a muffled drum
With fear to hear me come,

Now never sounds when I creep nigh.
Oh! she was always sly.

Yet if to spite her, I dared steal
Behind her bed, and feel

With fumbling fingers for her heart . . .
Ere I could touch the smart,

Once more wild shriek on shriek would tear
The dumb and shuddering air . . .

And still she never speaks to me.
She only smiles to see

How in dark corners secret-sly
New-born Eternity,

All spider-like, doth spin and cast
Strange threads to hold Time fast.

GOLD COAST CUSTOMS

To Helen Rootham

In Ashantee, a hundred years ago, the death of any rich or important person was followed by several days of national ceremonies, during which the utmost licence prevailed, and slaves and poor persons were killed that the bones of the deceased might be laved with human blood. These ceremonies were called Customs.

One fantee wave
Is grave and tall
As brave Ashantee's
Thick mud wall.
Munza rattles his bones in the dust,
Lurking in murk because he must.

Striped black and white
Is the squealing light;
The dust brays white in the market place,
Dead powder spread on a black skull's face.

Like monkey skin
Is the sea—one sin
Like a weasel is nailed to bleach on the rocks
Where the eyeless mud screeched fawning, mocks

At a negro that wipes
His knife . . . dug there
A bugbear bellowing
Bone dared rear—
A bugbear bone that bellows white
As the ventriloquist sound of light,

It rears at his head-dress of felted black hair
The one humanity clinging there—
His eyeless face whitened like black and white bones
And his beard of rusty
Brown grass cones.

Hard blue and white
Courie shells (the light
Grown hard) outline
The leopardskin musty
Leaves that shine
With an animal smell both thick and fusty.

One house like a ratskin
Mask flaps fleet
In the sailor's tall
Ventriloquist street
Where the rag houses flap—
Hiding a gap,

Here, tier on tier,
Like a black box rear
In the flapping slum
Beside Death's docks.
I did not know this meaner Death
Meant this: that the bunches of nerves still dance
And caper among these slums, and prance.

" Mariners, put your bones to bed! "
But at Lady Bamburger's parties each head,
Grinning, knew it had left its bones
In the mud with the white skulls . . . only the grin
Is left, strings of nerves, and the drum-taut skin.

When the sun in the empty
Sky is high
In his dirty brown and white
Birdskin dress—
He hangs like a skull
With a yellow dull
Face made of clay
(Where tainted, painted, the plague-spots bray)
To hide where the real face rotted away.

So our wormskin and paper masks still keep,
Above the rotting bones they hide,
The marks of the Plague whereof we died:
The belief,
The grief,
The love,
Or the grin
Of the shapeless worm-soft unshaping Sin—
Unshaping till no more the beat of the blood
Can raise up the body from endless mud
Though the hell-fires cold
As the worm, and old,
Are painted upon each unshaped form—
No more man, woman, or beast to see—
But the universal, devouring Worm.

When the sun of dawn looks down on the shrunken
Heads, drums of skin, and the dead men drunken,
I only know one half of my heart
Lies in that terrible coffin of stone,
My body that stalks through the slum alone.
And that half of my heart
That is in your breast

You gave for meat
In the sailor's street
To the rat that had only my bones to eat.

But those hardened hearts
That roll and sprawl,
In a cowl of foul blind monkey-skin,
Lest the whips of the light crash roaring in—
Those hearts that roll
Down the phantom street
They have for their beat
The cannibal drums
And the cries of the slums,
And the Bamburgher parties—they have them all!

One high house flaps . . . taps
Light's skin drum—
Monkey-like shrunk
On all fours now come
The parties' sick ghosts, each hunting himself—
Black gaps beneath an ape's thick pelt,

Chasing a rat,
Their soul's ghost fat
Through the negro swamp,
Slum hovel's cramp,
Of Lady Bamburgher's parties above
With the latest grin, and the latest love,
And the latest game:
To show the shame
Of the rat-fat soul to the grinning day
With even the ratskin flayed away.

Now, a thick cloud floating
Low o'er the lake,
Millions of flies
Begin to awake,
With the animation
Of smart conversation:
From Bedlam's madness the thick gadflies
Seek for the broken statue's eyes.

Where the mud and the murk
Whispering lurk:
" From me arises everything,
The negro's louse
The armadillo,
Munza's bone and his peccadillo,"

Where flaps degraded
The black and sated
Slack macerated
And antiquated
Beckoning negress
Nun of the shade,

And the rickety houses
Rock and rot,
Lady Bamburgher airs
That foul plague-spot
Her romantic heart.
From the cannibal mart,
That smart Plague-cart,
Lady Bamburgher rolls where the foul news-sheet
And the shambles for souls are set in the street.

And stuck in front
Of this world-tall Worm,
Stuck in front
Of this world's confession—
Like something rolled
Before a procession,
Is the face, a flimsy wormskin thing
That someone has raked
From the low plague-pit
As a figure-head
For Corruption dead,
And a mask for the universal Worm.

Her apeskin yellow
Tails of hair
Clung about her bone-white bare
Eyeless mask that cackled there:

The Worm's mask hid
Her eyeless mud,
Her shapeless love,
The plot to escape
From the God-ordained shape,

And her soul, the cannibal
Amazon's mart,
Where in squealing light
And clotted black night
On the monkey-skin black and white striped dust they
Cackle and bray
To the murdered day,

And the Amazon queen
With a bone-black face
Wears a mask with an apeskin beard; she grinds
Her male child's bones in a mortar, binds
Him for food, and the people buy. For this

Hidden behind
The Worm's mask grown
White as a bone
Where eyeholes rot wide
And are painted for sight,
And the little mouth red as a dead Plague-spot
On that white mask painted to hide Death's rot,

For this painted Plague-cart's
Heart, for this
Slime of the Worm that paints her kiss
And the dead men's bones round her throat and wrist,
The half of my heart that lay in your breast
Has fallen away
To rot and bray
With the painted mud through the eyeless day.

The dust of all the dead can blow
Backwards and forwards, to and fro
To cover the half of my heart with death's rot,
Yet the dust of that other half comes not
To this coffin of stone that stalks through the slum
Though love to you now is the deaf Worm's lust
That, cloven in halves, will reunite
Foulness to deadness in the dust
And chaos of the enormous night.

How far is our innocent paradise,
The blue-striped sand,
Bull-bellowing band
Of waves, and the great gold suns made wise
By the dead days and the horizons grand.

Can a planet tease
With its great gold train,
Walking beside the pompous main—
That great gold planet the heat of the Sun
Where we saw black Shadow, a black man, run,
So a negress dare
Wear long gold hair?
The negress Dorothy one sees
Beside the caverns and the trees
Where her parasol
Throws a shadow tall
As a waterfall—
The negress Dorothy still feels
The great gold planet tease her brain.

And dreaming deep within her blood
Lay Africa like the dark in the wood;
For Africa is the unhistorical
Unremembering, unrhetorical
Undeveloped spirit involved
In the conditions of nature—Man,
That black image of stone hath delved
On the threshold where history began.

Now under the cannibal
Sun is spread
The black rhinoceros-hide of the mud

For endlessness and timelessness . . . dead
Grass creaks like a carrion-bird's voice, rattles,
Squeaks like a wooden shuttle. Battles
Have worn this deserted skeleton black
As empty chain armour . . . lazily back
With only the half of its heart it lies,
With the giggling mud devouring its eyes,
Naught left to fight
But the black clotted night
In its heart, and ventriloquist squealing light.

But lying beneath the giggling mud
I thought there was something living, the bray
Of the eyeless mud can not betray—
Though it is buried beneath black bones
Of the fetiches screeching like overtones
Of the light, as they feel the slaves' spilt blood.

In tiers like a box
Beside the docks
The negro prays,
The negro knocks.
" Is anyone there ? "
His mumblings tear
Nothing but paper walls, and the blare
Of the gaping capering empty air.
The cannibal drums still roll in the mud
To the bones of the king's mother laved in blood
And the trophies with long black hair, shrunken heads
That drunken shrunk upon tumbled beds.

The negro rolls
His red eyeballs,

Prostrates himself.
The negro sprawls;
His God is but a flat black stone
Upright upon a squeaking bone.

The negro's dull
Red eyeballs roll. . . .
The immortality of the soul
Is but black ghosts that squeak through the hole
That once seemed eyes in Munza's skull.

This is his god:
The cannibal sun
On bones that played
For evermore,
And the rusty roar
Of the ancient Dead,
And the squealing rat
The soul's ghost fat.

So Lady Bamburgher's Shrunken Head,
Slum hovel, is full of the rat-eaten bones
Of a fashionable god that lived not
Ever, but still has bones to rot:
A bloodless and an unborn thing

That cannot wake, yet cannot sleep,
That makes no sound, that cannot weep,
That hears all, bears all, cannot move—
It is buried so deep
Like a shameful thing
In that plague-spot heart, Death's last dust-heap.

. . . . .

A tall house flaps
In the canvas street,
Down in the wineshop
The Amazons meet

With the tall abbess
Of the shade . . .
A ghost in a gown
Like a stiff brigade

Watches the sailor
With a guitar
Lure the wind
From the islands far.

Oh far horizons and bright blue wine
And majesty of the seas that shine,
Bull-bellowing waves that ever fall
Round the god-like feet and the goddess tall!

A great yellow flower
With the silence shy
To the wind from the islands
Sighs " I die."

At the foot of the steps
Like the navy-blue ghost
Of a coiling negro,
In dock slums lost,

(The ghost, haunting steamers
And cocktail bars,
Card-sharpers, schemers
And Pullman cars)

A ripple rose
With mud at its root
And weeping kissed
A statue's foot.

In the sailor's tall
Ventriloquist street
The calico dummies
Flap and meet;
Calculate: "Sally go
Pick up a sailor."
Behind that façade
The worm is a jailer.

"I cannot stiffen . . . I left my bones
Down in the street: no overtones
Of the murdered light can join my dust
To my black bones pressed in the House of Lust.
Only my feet still walk in the street;
But where is my heart and its empty beat?

Starved silly Sally, you dilly and dally,
The dummies said when I was a girl.
The rat deserts a room that is bare,
But Want, a cruel rat gnawing there
Ate to the heart, all else was gone,
Nothing remained but Want alone.
So now I'm a gay girl, a calico dummy,
With nothing left alive but my feet
That walk up and down in the Sailor's Street.

Behind the bawdy hovels like hoardings
Where harridans peer from the grovelling boarding
House, the lunatic
Wind still shakes
My empty rag-body, nothing wakes;
The wind like a lunatic in a fouled
Nightgown, whipped those rags and howled.

Once I saw it come
Through the canvas slum,
Rattle and beat what seemed a drum,
Rattle and beat it with a bone.
O Christ, that bone was dead, alone.
Christ, Who will speak to such ragged Dead
As me, I am dead, alone and bare,
They expose me still to the grinning air,
I shall never gather my bones and my dust
Together (so changed and scattered, lost . . .)
So I can be decently burièd.
What is that whimpering like a child
That this mad ghost beats like a drum in the air?
The heart of Sal
That once was a girl
And now is a calico thing to loll
Over the easy steps of the slum
Waiting for something dead to come."

From Rotten Alley and Booble Street,
The beggars crawl to starve near the meat
Of the reeling appalling cannibal mart
And Lady Bamburgher, smart Plague-cart.
Red rag face and a cough that tears
They creep through the mud of the docks from their
lairs;

And when the dog-whining dawn light
Nosed for their hearts, whined in fright,
With a sly high animal
Whimpering, half-frightened call
To worlds outside our consciousness
It finds no heart within their dress.
The Rat has eaten
That and beaten
Hope and love and memory,
At last, and even the will to die.
But what is the loss? For you cannot sell
The heart to those that have none for Hell
To fatten on . . . or that cheap machine,
And its beat would make springs for the dancing feet
Of Lady Bamburgher down in the street,
Of her dogs that nose out each other's sin,
And grin, and whine, and roll therein.

Against the Sea-wall are painted signs
" Here for a shilling a sailor dines."
Each Rag-and-Bone
Is propped up tall
(Lest in death it fall)
Against the Sea-wall.
Their empty mouths are sewed up whole
Lest from hunger they gape and cough up their soul.
The arms of one are stretched out wide . . .
How long, since our Christ was crucified?

Rich man Judas,
Brother Cain,
The rich men are your worms that gain

The air through seething from your brain;
Judas, mouldering in your old
Coffin body, still undying
As the Worm, where you are lying
With no flesh for warmth, but gold
For flesh, for warmth, for sheet,
Now you are fleshless, too, as these
That starve and freeze,
Is your gold hard as Hell's huge polar street,
Is the universal blackness of Hell's day so cold?

. . . . .

When, creeping over
The Sailor's street
Where the houses like ratskin
Masks flap, meet
Never across the murdered bone
Of the sailor, the whining overtone
Of dawn sounds, slaves
Rise from their graves,
Where in the corpse-sheet night they lay
Forgetting the mutilating day,
Like the unborn child in its innocent sleep.
Ah Christ, the murdered light must weep—
(Christ that takest away the sin
Of the world, and the rich man's bone-dead grin)
The light must weep
Seeing that sleep
And those slaves rise up in their death-chains, part
The light from the eyes
The hands from the heart,
Since their hearts are flesh for the tall
And sprawling
Reeling appalling

Cannibal mart,
But their hands and head
Are machines to breed
Gold for the old and the greedy Dead.

I have seen the murdered God look through the eyes
Of the drunkard's smirched
Mask as he lurched
O'er the half of my heart that lies in the street
Neath the dancing fleas and the foul news-sheet.

Where, a black gap flapping,
A white skin drum
The cannibal houses
Watch this come—
Lady Bamburgher's party; for the plan
Is a prize for those that on all fours ran
Through the rotting slum
Till those who come
Could never guess from the mudcovered shapes
Which are the rich or the mired dire apes
As they run where the souls, dirty paper, are blown
In the hour before dawn, through this long hell of
stone.

Perhaps if I too lie down in the mud,
Beneath tumbrils rolling
And mad skulls galloping
Far from their bunches of nerves that dance
And caper among these slums and prance,
Beneath the noise of that hell that rolls
I shall forget the shrunken souls
The eyeless mud squealing " God is dead,"

Starved men (bags of wind), and the harlot's tread,
The heaven turned into monkey-hide
By Lady Bamburgher's dancing fleas,
Her rotting parties and death-slack ease,
And the dead men drunken
(The only tide)
Blown up and down
And tossed through the town
Over the half of my heart that lies,
Deep down, in this meaner Death with cries.

The leaves of black hippopotamus-hide
Black as the mud
Cover the blood
And the rotting world. Do we smell and see

That sick thick smoke from London burning,
Gomorrah turning
Like worms in the grave,
The Bedlam daylights murderous roar,
Those pillars of fire the drunkard and whore,
Dirty souls boiled in cannibal cookshops to paper
To make into newspapers, flags? . . . They caper
Like gaping apes. Foul fires we see,
For Bedlam awakes to reality.

The drunken burning,
The skin drums galloping,
In their long march still parched for the sky,
The Rotten Alleys where beggars groan
And the beggar and his dog share a bone;
The rich man Cain that hides within
His lumbering palaces where Sin

Through the eyeless holes of Day peers in,
The murdered heart that all night turns
From small machine to shapeless Worm
With hate, and like Gomorrah burns—
These put the eyes of Heaven out,
These raise all Hell's throats to a shout,
These break my heart's walls toppling in,
And like a universal sea
The nations of the Dead crowd in.

Bahunda, Banbangala, Barumbe, Bonge,
And London fall . . . rolling human skin drums
Surrounded by long black hair, I hear
Their stones that fall,
Their voices that call,
Among the black and the bellowing bones.

But yet when the cannibal
Sun is high
The sightless mud
Weeps tears, a sigh,
To rhinoceros-hided leaves: "Ah why
So sightless, earless, voiceless, I?"

The mud has at least its skulls to roll;
But here as I walk, no voices call,
Only the stones and the bones that fall;
But yet if only one soul would whine,
Rat-like from the lowest mud, I should know
That somewhere in God's vast love it would shine;
But even the rat-whine has guttered low.

I saw the Blind like a winding-sheet
Tossed up and down through the blind man's street
Where the dead plague-spot
Of the spirit's rot
On the swollen thick houses
Cries to the quick,
Cries to the dark soul that lies there and dies
In hunger and murk, and answers not.

Gomorrah's fires have washed my blood—
But the fires of God shall wash the mud
Till the skin drums rolling
The slum cries sprawling
And crawling
Are calling
" Burn thou me! "
Though Death has taken
And pig-like shaken
Rooted and tossed
The rags of me.
Yet the time will come
To the heart's dark slum
When the rich man's gold and the rich man's wheat
Will grow in the street, that the starved may eat,—
And the sea of the rich will give up its dead—
And the last blood and fire from my side will be shed.
For the fires of God go marching on.

NOTES

" The Negroes indulge that perfect contempt for humanity which in its bearing on Justice and Morality is the fundamental characteristic of the race. They have, moreover, no knowledge of the immortality of the soul, although spectres are supposed to appear. The undervaluing of humanity among them reaches an incredible degree of intensity. Tyranny is regarded as no wrong, and cannibalism is looked upon as quite customary and proper. Among us instinct deters from it, if we can speak of instinct at all as appertaining to man. But with the Negro this is not the case, and the devouring of human flesh is altogether consonant with the general principles of the African race; to the sensual Negro, human flesh is but an object of sense—mere flesh. At the death of a king hundreds are killed and eaten; prisoners are butchered and their flesh sold in the market-place; the victor is accustomed to eat the flesh of his fallen foe."—HEGEL'S "Philosophy of History."

Page 265: "Munza rattles his bones in the dust." King Munza reigned, in 1874, over the Monbuttoo, a race of cannibals in Central Africa. These notes are taken from Dr. Georg Schweinfurth's "The Heart of Africa" (translated by Ellen Frewer, published by Messrs. Sampson Low). Of the Monbuttoo and their neighbours the Niam-Niam, we read: "Human fat is universally sold. . . . Should any lone and solitary individual die, uncared for . . . he would be sure to be devoured in the very district in which he lived. During our residence at the court of Munza the general rumour was quite current that nearly every day some little child was sacrificed to supply his meal. There are cases in which bearers who died from fatigue had been dug out of the graves in which they had been buried . . . in order that they might be devoured. The cannibalism of the Monbuttoo is the most pronounced of all the known nations of Africa. Surrounded as they are by a number of people who, being inferior to them in culture, are consequently held in great contempt, they have just the opportunity which they want for carrying on expeditions of war and plunder, which result in the acquisition of a booty which is especially coveted by them, consisting of human flesh. But with it all, the Monbuttoos are a noble race of men, men who display a certain national pride . . . men to whom one may put a reasonable question and receive a reasonable answer. The Nubians can never say enough in praise of their faithfulness in friendly intercourse and of the order and stability of their national life. According to the Nubians, too, the Monbuttoos were their superiors in the arts of war."

Any traveller from Monbuttoo visiting first of all our new "Original Parties" and then walking down the Embankment, or in those streets of Revue Theatres, where our late heroes sell matches in the gutter, could not fail to be impressed by the superiority of our civilization over that of the Monbuttoos.

Page 270, *line* 22 : " And her soul, the cannibal Amazon's mart."

" Tradition alleges that in former times a state composed of women made itself famous by its conquests : it was a state at whose head was a woman. She is said to have pounded her own son in a mortar, and to have had the blood of pounded children constantly at hand. She is said to have driven away or put to death all the males, and commanded the death of all male children. These furies destroyed everything in the neighbourhood, and were driven to constant plunderings because they did not cultivate the land . . . This infamous state, the report goes on to say, subsequently disappeared."—HEGEL's " Philosophy of History," chapter on Africa.

[illegible]

[illegible]
Tartars, and that warlike [illegible]
of [illegible], where [illegible]
[illegible]
over that of the [illegible].

[illegible]
[illegible]
[illegible]
a woman. She is said to have murdered her own son [illegible]
and to have had the [illegible]
she is said to have [illegible]
[illegible]
[illegible]
[illegible]
[illegible]
Philosophy of [illegible]